Ireland

- Judge James Johnston Shaw 1845-1910 — Mary Elizabeth Maxwell 1842-1908
  - Margaret (Meg) Shaw 1872-1949
  - Rowan Shaw 1880-1916
  - Billy Shaw 1882-1917

- Thornley Woods 1897-1916
- John Lowe (Jack) Woods 1899-1956
- Robert Rowan (Bobby) Woods 1902-1971 — Patricia Proctor 1904-1977

- Elizabeth Alston 1926-2006
- Dorothy Dunlop 1929-Present

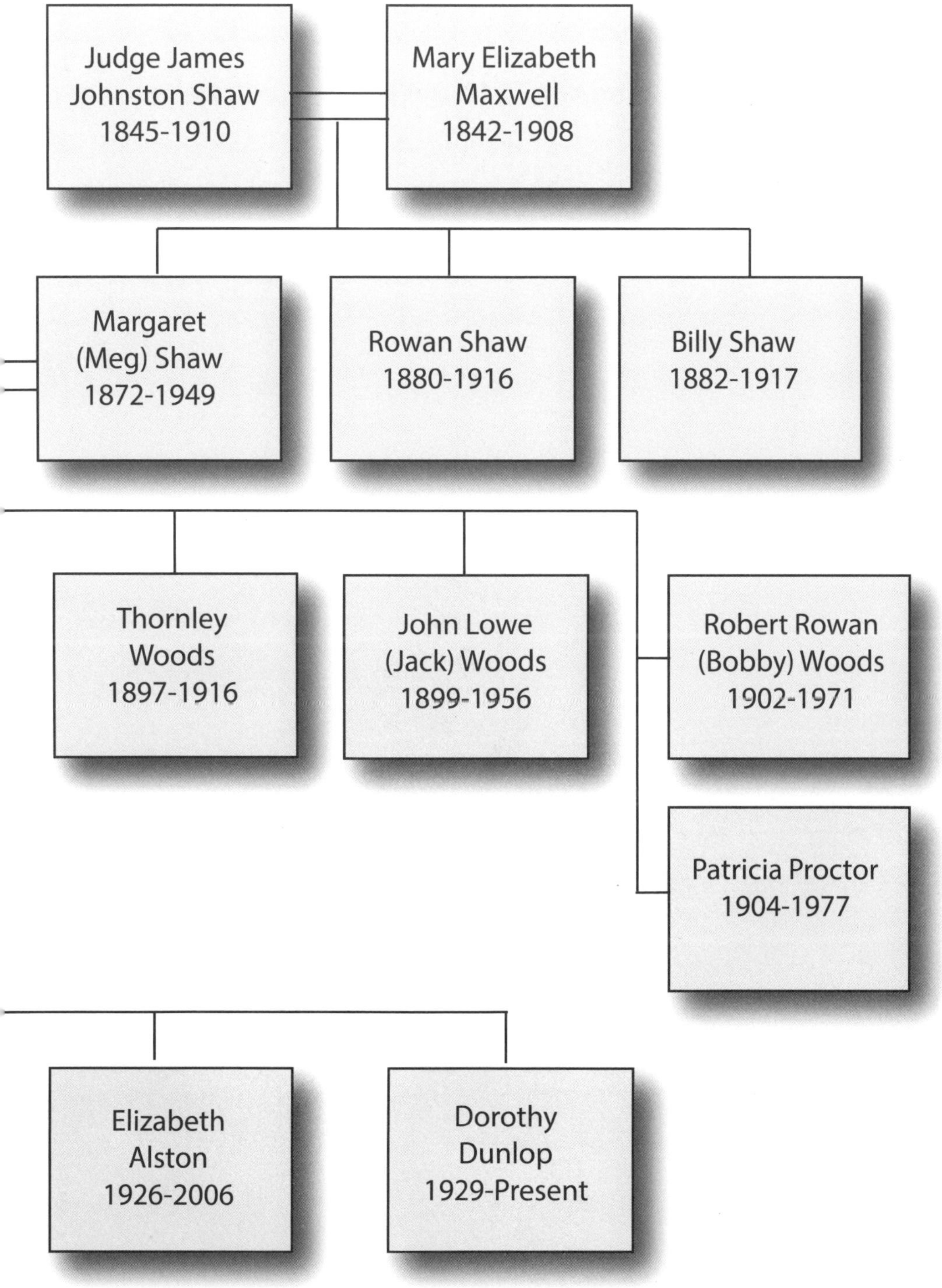

1916
and
Beyond
the Pale

Dorothy Dunlop

First published in April 2016

Publisher: Motelands Publishing

© 2016 Dorothy Dunlop

All rights reserved. No part of this publication may be reproduced, stored in a retrieval system, or transmitted, in any form, or by any means, electronic, mechanical, photocopying, recording or otherwise, without the prior permission of the publisher and copyright holder.

ISBN 978-0-9934434-2-8

Printed and bound by
CPI Group (UK) Ltd, Croydon, CR0 4YY

Cover by Ptarmigan Design

Acknowledgements

First of all I wish to thank my immediate family, Patricia, Gilbert, Hugh and Miranda for their unswerving support in the research into the family history and the discovery of long hidden letters and photographs and finally with the editing and production of this book. I thank also my nieces, Ana Golub and Jacqui Chaddock, for their contributions of letters and photographs, and I particularly want to acknowledge the groundwork undertaken by Mark Hely-Hutchinson in reviewing the Woods letters. I also wish to extend my gratitude to my cousin Robert Woods and his wife Ann for their help and interest, and the recording of our Aunt Patricia's memories of her childhood.

I am totally indebted to J.W.O. Morrison for being my publisher, and his belief that this is a story that will touch many heartstrings from Dublin to Dunedin, wherever the huge sacrifices of World War I are commemorated.

I also thank Gordon Brand, Stephen Stanford, John Erskine, Niall Hannigan and Sinclair Duncan for their help and advice.

Contents

Introduction

1 **Chapter I: Summer 1914**
Gilbert Waterhouse in Germany at the Outbreak of War

7 **Chapter II: 1914 - April 1916**
Woods family correspondence between Dublin and France

67 **Chapter III: Dublin Easter Rising**
First-hand account from Molly Woods

83 **Chapter IV: June 1916 - 1918**
"All Men Must Die"

103 **Chapter V: Gilbert in Trinity College**
Letters from his family 1914-1918

149 **Chapter VI: Allied Naval Armistice Commission Inspection of the German Navy**
Second Lieutenant Officer Gilbert Waterhouse aboard H.M.S. Hercules

163 **Chapter VII: The Aftermath and the Survivors**

Appendices and Bibliography

In memory of all those who fell in battle in World Wars I and II

"Fertility, Sterility, Futility"

Warm are the winds of heaven,
    Sweet are the songs of spring,
But men from light are riven,
    When War is on the wing.
The bluest skies are shuttered
    And the reddest sun must rise
Behind the banners fluttered
    Before our squinting eyes.

The autumn seed shall prosper
    When the earth is rich and good,
The winds that softest whisper
    Shall quickest clothe the wood;
So are our children dearest,
    Fairest in mind and form,
Whom Peace shall nurture nearest,
    Abundance shield from storm.

But winter's winds shall wither,
    Siberia's snows shall swamp,
When War's dread blast draws hither
    To strike the windswept camp.
When Freedom's captured daughters
    O'er her mangled sons shall weep
When mourn the stormy waters
    Above the glutted deep.

And when War's wingflap searing
    On its scorching way has passed,
And have gone beyond all hearing
    The echoes of its blast,
The victor and the vanquished
    Shall dig each barren grave,
And think with senses anguished
    "We destroyed, that we might save!"

Written by Dorothy c. 1943

Introduction

This is the story of two young people, born under the same flag but in two very different cultures, who, unknown to each other at the time, lived out the turbulent and momentous years of the First World War barely half a mile apart.

My father, Gilbert Waterhouse, was born of comparatively humble stock, his father Harold being a clerk in the Lancashire and Yorkshire Railway. But by dint of winning a scholarship to the Manchester Grammar School, Gilbert in due course graduated with distinction in languages from St. John's College, Cambridge, and in 1914, after some time teaching in Germany, had just been appointed Professor of German in Trinity College, Dublin.

The same year, my mother, Mary Elizabeth Woods, went up to Newnham College, Cambridge, as a fresher in English and Anglo-Saxon Studies. Her father, Sir Robert Woods, had also made the jump from an obscure rural background in Co. Offaly to becoming a well-known E.N.T. surgeon in Dublin. His consulting rooms and family home were at 39 Merrion Square, with a country retreat in Killiney, Co. Dublin.

It is easy to see that their talents and love of languages and the arts made these two ideal companions when they finally met and married after the Great War. This is the story of what happened to their two families from the outbreak of war, told entirely in the letters and accounts which survive, set in the background of dark and dire days in Dublin and the trenches of France.

Dorothy Dunlop
April 2016

Chapter I

1914
Gilbert Waterhouse in Germany at the Outbreak of War

Gilbert Waterhouse was the elder son of Harold and Sarah Helen Waterhouse. He was born in Hipperholme, Yorkshire on the 15th July 1888, and went to the Manchester Grammar School and St. John's College, Cambridge. He spent 1911-1914 teaching at Leipzig University, and was holidaying in Germany during the summer vacation of 1914. This chapter describes his hazardous exit from Germany just before War was declared.

Memoir recorded on July 28th 1969

My recollection of days and dates is a little hazy. My last letter, dated July 26th 1914, says that I expected to be home on Wednesday afternoon, August 5th. *Whitaker's Almanac* tells me that we were at war with Germany on August 4th. I will assume for the moment that our ultimatum to Germany expired at midnight on Monday, August 3rd., which would fit in with the story I have always told, viz. that I 'got out' of Germany on August 1st., which was a Saturday. Anyway, on the evening of Sunday, July 26th (I believe), I had supper with Professor Jaeger (Law) and, I think, two other professors, in the restaurant at the Palmengarten (Botanic Gardens). During the evening the waiter came excitedly to our table and said, 'Die Russen haben die österreichische Grenze überschritten': (The Russians have crossed the Austrian frontier'), whereupon Professor Jaeger commented, 'Dann ist der Bündnisfall gegeben' (Then the alliance comes into operation). This appeared to mean that Germany was automatically at war with Russia and, almost certainly, with France. That the report was not true made little difference in the end. Our little party broke up on a gloomy note.

I must have been a singularly naïve and unsuspecting young man not to have seen what the effects of the assassination of the Archduke Franz Ferdinand were likely to be. All Leipzig, and indeed all Germany, was buzzing with indignation but my own reaction was, 'Why all this fuss?' It was a foul murder and Austria was fully justified in demanding condign punishment of the criminals, but why war? What had it to do with Germany anyway and with Leipzig in particular, where life was so settled and pleasant? All this talk of war seemed so unnecessary, even stupid.

What first gave me cause for alarm was an entertainment in a large Beer Hall some days before the evening above-mentioned. There had been an international wrestling competition and the four finalists were now wrestling for the championship. They were: an Italian, a Frenchman, a German and a Serb. They were all magnificent men of about 14-15 stone, the Frenchman being distinctly the fattest and probably the heaviest. The hall was packed, the spectators watching the bouts while eating and drinking at the tables on the floor. It was the first really noisy and potentially violent gathering I had ever attended in Germany. In due course, the Italian and the Frenchman were beaten, leaving the German, a Bavarian named Bauer, and the Serb to face one another in the final. Both were fine men and, as far as I could judge, scrupulously fair in their tactics, but it was now, for the first time, that I really understood what the Sarajevo murder meant for world politics. The Serb was treated to a continuous bellow of insult and abuse from the now frantic audience, the favourite epithet being apparently 'Hammeldieb' (sheep-stealer). The German wore a vest but the Serb was stripped to the waist and for some reason or other the hostile spectators thought this made him slippery and not easy to hold. They kept on yelling: 'Trikotanziehen: Trikotanziehen', until the master of ceremonies came forward and assured them that Bauer did not want his opponent to wear a vest. It was a very even contest but I thought the German just the stronger of the two. Anyway, the Serb had the good fortune, or the good sense, to lose. He would have been murdered by the mob if he had won. This incident opened my eyes and the next day I withdrew all my money, about 300 M, from the bank and carried it in a bag round my neck pending my departure.

On the Thursday before the outbreak of war, Mr. Kent, the American Consul, myself, and one or two Germans, were guests at dinner with a Mr. Doering, a German-American who had spent most of his life in the United States. He had retired to Leipzig, his birthplace, a year or so ago and had taken a prominent part in the social affairs of the American colony. We became more or less partners in the organization of Anglo-American dances and theatricals and got on very well together. Later, I learned from Captain Francis Quarry, who escaped from Leipzig by a clever trick after the outbreak of war, that the genial Mr. Doering was a German police spy and that his job was to watch the Anglo-American colony from the inside. When war came, the American Consulate accepted the diplomatic responsibility for protecting the interests of such British subjects, such as my Irish friend, Captain Quarry, as still remained, and the unsuspecting Mr. Kent, requiring additional staff, appointed Mr. Doering, as an assistant, and Mr. Doering, of course, passed to the German police such information about Consular business as he thought would be useful to them.

The dinner was excellent, the conversation intelligent and it was agreed that, as far as the political situation was concerned, the visit of Prince Henry of Prussia to London must have removed any danger of war.

Some weeks previously, I had promised Mr. Kent, who was interested in Luther and places associated with him, that I would arrange my route back to England so that I could accompany him to places like Worms and Speier. He had been transferred from Peking to Leipzig and while I believe he was fluent in Chinese, he knew no German. He was a man I had quickly grown to like and respect and as I was leaving Germany for good, and as the detour was through country I did not know very well, I was interested to explore it. We were to be accompanied by a young Mr. Lansing, a nephew, I think, of the then Secretary of State in Washington.

If my dates are correct, it was about ten o'clock on the morning of Friday, July 31st that we took the train from Leipzig to Mainz. We were an hour or so late in Frankfort and were surprised to see soldiers posted here and there by the track and sidings as we ran in. We had to change; there was much confusion and crowding in the station but as nobody seemed to be able to explain the presence of the military, we pushed on to Mainz, arriving there about six. We went to the nearest small hotel opposite the station, secured rooms, and then took a walk in the direction of the river. We had not gone far before we saw a small crowd gathering round a hoarding, where a man was pasting up a notice. It read 'GENERAL MOBILIZATION'. I explained it to my companions and we returned to the hotel and asked the proprietor what it all meant. He tried to reassure us, saying that it was only manoeuvres and that everything would be normal in a day or two if we stayed where we were. Luckily, I was not in the least reassured and I told my friends that even if it were only 'manoeuvres', the army would probably monopolize the railways and, as far I was concerned, I was going home at once. Thereupon, I went to the station, found that the Flushing boat-train was scheduled to leave at 2.34 a.m., bought a 2nd class ticket, checked my trunk through to London and returned to the hotel. Mr. Kent said that if things were really as serious as I thought, he felt he ought to go back to his post in Leipzig. I said that was for him to decide, but I was certainly going home by the first available train. We had a meal together and about ten o'clock I saw them off back to Leipzig.

Meanwhile, I had noticed an occasional batch of young men, in civilian clothes, marching to the station and I assumed that they had been called up and were on their way to a depot.

It was lonely in the hotel after my friends had gone, so about midnight I took my two suitcases and found a seat on the platform. At first, I was almost alone but gradually more and more passengers gathered as trains came in and were emptied to the order 'All change'. The Flushing boat train, due at 2.34, did not arrive until 4.30 and during the long wait I had become more and more anxious. When I opened the door of the through coach, people almost fell out on to the platform, it was so full. It was impossible to get in but having noticed, as the train came in, that the leading coach was labelled 'Amsterdam III Klasse' I thought it would suit me well enough. Hurrying forward, I managed to plant my suitcases in the corridor and sat on them all night.

We stopped several times. No doubt some passengers got out, but more got in. At Bonn, I remember seeing a party of English schoolgirls looking anxiously for places; I think they all got in. At Wesel, we were hopelessly late for our connection with the Berlin-Flushing portion of the train. After some time we were attached to a local and trundled slowly from station to station - one of them was Xanten, the birthplace of Siegfried - until we reached the frontier at Goch. Here we were all turned out but the Dutch had a train waiting and we all climbed in. This time there were seats for all. Then came the German police, checking passports and tickets. Fortunately, we English had not yet become enemies and the police were quite friendly. Perhaps it had not yet occurred to them that England would go to war if Belgium were invaded. Anyway, even passports were not absolutely necessary for foreign travel in those days. I had the impression that the police were not so much interested in foreigners as in those of their fellow-countrymen as might be leaving Germany to avoid military service.

At length, the train was cleared and we rumbled across the Maas Bridge, out of Germany into Holland. Somebody said it was already prepared for demolition, should the Germans invade Holland. I can still feel the sigh of relief when we saw the first Dutch sentry. I cannot remember whether we had had time for a snack at Goch; I rather think I had eaten nothing since supper in Mainz and obtained nothing until I reached Flushing.

Soon, a new note of anxiety was sounded; the Dutch had mobilized, too. At larger stations, such as Tilburg, coaches filled with troops were attached to the train, thus adding to the slowness of our progress. The Dutch soldiers struck me as a weedy, undersized lot compared with the stalwart Germans and I felt that they would be easily brushed aside, should Holland be invaded.

We reached Flushing eight hours too late for the day-boat but in comfortable time for the night sailing. I secured a berth, had supper and went to my cabin, where I was soon joined by a Dutch passenger. We slept well and when daylight came my fellow-traveller woke and asked, 'Is this Folkestone?' to which I replied, 'We haven't started yet'. There had been none of the noise and vibration one associates with a Channel crossing and there we were, still at Flushing pier. However, we did start and reached Folkestone without incident.

I suppose it was about two o'clock when the boat train reached Victoria. My tin trunk was not in the van. Somebody suggested it might have gone to Holborn viaduct, so I put my suitcases in the Left Luggage Office and went to Holborn. The trunk was not there.

I decided to try Victoria again in the evening and spent the rest of the afternoon at Hampton Court, which I had never seen. It must have been eight or nine o'clock when I returned to Victoria to meet the next scheduled service from Folkestone or Dover, should there be one: There was. About three hundred passengers alighted but there were only seventeen pieces of luggage in the van. I counted them; my trunk was not among them. As a forlorn hope, I decided to leave my name and address, with a description of the trunk, at the Customs Office in the station. I handed the particulars to the clerk-in-charge and to my great surprise, he said, 'I think that came last night.' He took me inside and, sure enough, there it was: somewhat battered and with the lid rather loose. A helpful porter removed a rope from somebody else's trunk, tied it round mine, called a cab, and away I went to Euston to catch the midnight train to Manchester.

It was between seven and eight on the Monday morning when I reached Heywood. My father was walking in the garden, already half convinced that I had been trapped in Germany. About an hour later, the Lancashire and Yorkshire van drove up and delivered the heavy box of books and papers that I had dispatched from Leipzig by fast freight some three weeks before.

Chapter II

1914 - April 1916
Woods family correspondence between Dublin and France

Sir Robert and Lady Woods lived in 39 Merrion Square where Sir Robert, an E.N.T. specialist, had his home and consulting rooms. Robert Woods was born at Tullamore on April 27th, 1865. His father, Christopher Woods was descended from a Lancashire ancestor, who came to Ireland at the time of the Commonwealth. His mother was a daughter of James Lowe of Westmeath. Like many other distinguished professional men, he received his early education at Wesley College, Dublin, and after graduating at Trinity College and further study in surgery in Vienna, he set up his own practice. He represented Trinity College at Westminster from 1918-1922, taking part in the Mansion House Conference of 1922, which led ultimately to the treaty of Downing Street.

My memories of my grandfather are clear but always tinged slightly by a childish fear of what he might say next to tease me, as he loved to probe my small mind or test me with practical jokes. My favourite times with him were spent in his workshop, watching his skill as he moulded little busts of family members or carved with intricate tools. Perhaps he was also then at his most relaxed. At other times he could be stern and exacting with his family. I felt very proud one day when comparing my stubby hands to the long fingers of my sisters, my aunt Patricia remarked kindly, "Oh, but you have your grandfather's hands."

Born in 1895, their eldest child, Mary Elizabeth (Molly) Woods was a student at Newnham College, Cambridge. Her three brothers, Thornley, Jack and Bobby were at Shrewsbury School and her young sister, Patsy, was at home. In the summer Thornley enlisted straight from the Officers Training Corps and followed his two maternal uncles, Rowan and Billy Shaw to France In 1915.

Rowan and William Shaw were younger brothers to Lady Woods, born Margaret Gamble Maxwell Shaw. Her father, Judge James Johnston Shaw, was a descendant of the Shaws who had been granted land by Hugh Montgomerie during the plantation of the Ards Peninsula, and his daughter, fondly known as Meg, was brought up in the strict Presbyterianism of Kircubbin, her close relations being the Ulster Scots families of Gamble and Maxwell, her mother being Mary Elizabeth Maxwell of Ballyherley, Portferry. The Shaw family grave is in the old churchyard of Greyabbey.

Rowan Shaw, who had studied Law, left Ireland in 1908 to join a Solicitors' Office in the Malay States, based in Ipoh, Perak, where the Cowdys of Co. Down were his partners. After qualifying in Law, my mother's brother Jack also joined this firm, and lived to be a prisoner of the Japanese in WWII. In 1914, Rowan enlisted in the Cheshire Regiment.

The younger brother, Billy, had already chosen to be a regular soldier, and sailed for India in March 1908. Judge Shaw never saw his sons again. He died in 1910.

The uncles, Rowan and Billy Shaw, being unmarried and away from Ireland for long periods, regarded their sister Margaret's home in 39 Merrion Square as their own, much to the delight of the young Woods's.

Rowan was full of fun and ready for any games, while Billy was quieter and more responsible, but both were much loved.

In the happy and peaceful times of 1913, Billy wrote to his sister from Chester where he was stationed.

June 6th, 1913: Billy to Meg
The Castle, Chester

My dear Megsie,

I was awfully pleased when I saw Robert's name in the Honours List. I congratulate you both most heartily. It must be a great pleasure to you, as indeed it is to all of us, that Robert's position in his profession should receive the cachet of official recognition and it must be equally pleasant that you, as his wife, participate in this distinction. To me, as your brother, it is of course of especial gratification and without any pain, as you put it. I can honestly say that I congratulate you both on achieving a distinction that you both thoroughly deserve.

Ever since I played gooseberry to you many years ago I have always felt that you backed the right horse when you married Robert and now he has succeeded in making you a lady I feel it even more (forgive this little jibe). You know what I mean. I know that neither of you ever cared much one way or the other about these things and I don't suppose to anyone who knows either of you it can in any way affect the estimate of you they already hold, but still to a man like Robert who has by sheer ability risen from the bottom to the top of his profession it cannot be regarded as a mere formal and empty honour but as a very real and grateful tribute to his genius from sovereign and fellow-countrymen more especially as it has come quite unsolicited. My one regret at this moment is that father is not alive as I know how highly he esteemed and appreciated Robert and what intense pleasure he would have received from seeing his daughter and son-in-law officially honoured.

Ever your loving brother, Billy.

September 7th 1914: Billy to Meg
1 Royal Terrace, Northampton

My dear Megsie,

I am at last enabled to snatch a moment to write to you. The above will be my address until further notice. The whole of the Welsh Division is concentrated here. I am at last able to give you some definite news. All the terriers who have volunteered for active service have been formed into three Army Corps called the Central Force under the command of Sir Ian Hamilton. We belong to the 1st Army under the command of Sir Bruce Hamilton and our division (the Welsh) is part of it. The idea is that we should stay here training, they expect us to be ready in three months and then the whole force will be shifted to the Continent according as the strategic situation requires and act as a 2nd Army. So I don't suppose we shall get a biff at the Germans till about the end of November. We are all working 18 hours a day to get these fellows trained and ready. We are billeted here (16,000) in private houses and all over the place, this palatial residence is my office and is the best address for letters. It is a small suburban villa in a style that reproduce themselves with unfailing regularity all over the town.

I got Robert's letter about Thornley having brought my things over to Ireland. I wish you would get Thornley to write to me and tell me more or less what he left behind in my lodgings so I can make arrangements to have them stored, also to let me know if he ever got the big trunk that I ordered to be sent from my London club to Chester. I trust the pup is going strong and behaving himself. Give him my love. I should like you to put naphthalene or something of the sort with my clothes, so that the moth and rust will not corrupt or the thieves break through and steal. I will try and write more regularly in future as things are now getting more or less settled. You had better regard the information I gave you in the first part of this letter as confidential as we are not supposed to let anyone know of our movements or organisation. These casualty lists are terrible, a lot of my pals have been killed and wounded but these things must be.

Love to all at home, ever your Billy.

July 10th, 1915: Billy to Robert

I'm afraid I can't possibly tell you where I am except that it is in the forefront of the battle where they will hardly allow you to come. The last time I heard of the leader of the -----bo's, however, he was somewhere near Fricourt. Thornley is somewhere near at hand on the left. Hope you will have a cheery trip. Everything is going well here and we have got them on the run.

In great haste, Yours ever, Billy.

August 29th, 1915: Billy to Robert

We have at last arrived here, but I am not allowed to tell you where. We had a very comfortable journey. We left Bordon about 10 and railed to Southampton, where we embarked on a huge liner and crossed that night, we all had to wear life-belts, and everyone was warned about submarines.

We had to anchor outside the harbour to wait for the tide, and when they let go the anchor all the men thought we had been torpedoed, I never saw them get up a companion quicker, it was the funniest thing in the world, led by a fat sergt-major. We arrived at Havre and stayed at a rest camp for the night, and next day (Friday) we entrained and travelled for 24 hours, and here we are. Everything was very comfortable and very well organised. We are now in billets, and it is most amusing to hear the men talking French. Some of them are amazed that it is possible for a human being not to understand English

The last two days have been very hot, but it is raining to-day.

September 2nd, 1915: Billy to Meg

Things are very quiet out here at present, and the weather is vile. It has been raining hard all day to-day, and it looks like going on for some time; a peasant whom I asked in my flowing French said 5 days probably, luckily my sword was at Rathleigh or I would have stuck him with it. I did not consider the case serious enough to waste a revolver cartridge on. My flow of idiomatic French surprises me as much as it does the natives!

September 3rd, 1915: Billy to Meg

I received your letter yesterday, also the snapshots which are very good especially of the pup, I am keeping them. I am sending you two taken of the King's inspection parade before we embarked, one of me on "Slim Jim" my first charger, he's a beautiful horse, but unfortunately has to be dyed a dirty yellow colour, as a grey "est très conspicué pour les Boches," my second charger is a chestnut polo pony, I am sending Bobby a p.c. of him. The other snapshot is a back view of me on the same parade with a Major Badham-Thornhill, a Galway man. My groom is up in the p.c. of "Susan." I wonder if you would keep all these photos, and anything else of interest like newspaper cuttings that you get from me together in a box or somewhere, as they will be rather an interesting record of the War. I heard my first shot fired in anger on Sept 2nd, 1915 at 11.10 a.m., I noted the time carefully, luckily it was nowhere near me. Things seem to be very quiet here at present, though it's awfully hard to find out what's going on, the French seem to be fighting very hard in the Argonne, they all think, (the French people, I mean) that the War will be over in December, but I don't see how that's possible. December year is nearer it.

We are at present in what is called general reserve, and are billeted in a village; apart from the extremely wet weather we are comfortable enough. I spend any spare time I have in talking French, and am coming on as a conversationalist rapidly, it's wonderful how quickly one gets back the little one ever knew. They issue us with a ration of tobacco, judge of my horror when I discovered it was Irish, so I am getting 100 cigarettes, the same as you used to smoke, and ¼ lb mild smoking mixture sent out from Mitchell every fortnight. I hope Thornley will get his Commission in the R.F.A.[1] all right, but he need be in no hurry to come out here, as far as I can gather it will last some little time yet. Do you know where Rowan is? I got a letter from him before I left saying he was just going to Whitchurch and I wrote to him there, but Molly tells me in her letter that he is still in St. Asaph hunting escaped German prisoners. Thornley had better use my sword, as he will want one at home for drill purposes, and it would be absurd to buy one, as they are of no use at all out here. So he ought to try and get his riding

---

[1] Royal Field Artillery

finished before he joins, as he will have to devote all his time to learning the gunnery job afterwards, it has become a very exact science, even during this War.

September 9th, 1915: Billy to Meg

I'm afraid I have not written to you for some time, but I have really not had a moment till now. I have so much to tell you that I doubt if I can get it all into one letter. First of all, the shirts arrived all right… We moved from our last place on Monday 6th, and marched about 25 miles, and then billeted for the night. The weather, by the way, has been perfect ever since we moved. Next morning Tuesday, we were off at dawn, and marched another 20 miles behind the line and billeted again. Our billets were French farmhouses and very comfortable. On Tuesday, on the march, I met Eric Hammond and that night he motored out to my billet, brought me in, gave me an excellent dinner, and motored me out again. He has got a ripping good job, and lives like a Duke in a Chateau, well away from the firing line. He assured me we were going to be kept in reserve for some time, so I ate and drank heartily, and motored back full of good cheer and looking forward to a quiet time.

When I got back orders were waiting that Battery Commanders were to go out at 6 a.m. next morning to reconnoitre positions. The good cheer at once oozed out at every pore, and I got into my little flea-bag with a sinking sensation where once a good dinner had been. Next morning, in the middle of the night, I crawled out again, trifled with a cup of lukewarm tea, climbed on to my horse, and started out. At the rendezvous I met three other cheap looking B.C.s[2] and we cross-examined each other closely to see if we all had the requisite instruments, maps, compasses etc., to knock out the wily Hun. Thornhill, the man from Galway, caused the first bright spot in the morning by exclaiming at the end of the cross-examination, "Well, thank God, I've got a drop of whiskey anyhow," which made me laugh consumedly. From the rendezvous we rode up and met our General, who turned out to be to my great delight, George Carey, my oldest friend. He greeted me warmly, and told us we were to bring our batteries into action that night, each of us to take over a position from another battery, which was moving out that night into reserve. He showed us on the map where we would find the batteries we were relieving, and told me to come back when I had seen the place and lunch with him. So off we started again, Thornhill and I had to go very close to each other. And on our way we passed through a large town absolutely ruined by shell (I am not allowed to tell you its name) and intermittent shell falling into it then. We found an Estaminet[3], and dug an old woman out of the cellar, and had a bottle of vin rouge to hearten us on our way, it was a frightfully hot day. We then went on, on foot, about a mile, with shots dropping all round us, and found our respective batteries. I found that the B.C. I was taking

---

[2] Battery Commanders
[3] A small café bar

over from was Arthur Leech, with whom I was at school, so I met a lot of old friends. He had a beautiful dugout in position, the guns absolutely covered, and a splendid funk-hole for himself, in which I am writing this now. He took me all round, and showed us everything, including a most excellent telephone exchange in a dug-out, and I then walked back (of course one can't ride up anywhere near the firing line) to the afore-mentioned town and picked up Carey's car (one side riddled with shrapnel) and motored back to R.A. Headqrs and lunched with Carey. After lunch he took me for a drive round behind most of his line, which was very interesting, and then I went back to Leech's battery. Leech then took me down to the front line trench, from which we observe our fire when there is an attack on. This was a most thrilling experience, and fairly put the heart across me. We left the battery position, and walked across some fields into a communication trench, and then up this trench into the front trench. It was terrible and terrifying the first time you do it. And I had just screwed up my courage to have a look over, when a Royal Irish Rifleman said, "I wouldn't look there, sir, they've just hit that sandbag, it's a bit dangerous" – I thanked him profusely, and moved on a bit, and had my first close view of the German trenches. I didn't see as much as the top of a hat, but as they were only 40 yards away that's hardly surprising. We then walked along the front trench to our regular observing station. This is a house just behind our front lines, which has already had the roof knocked off it, and several holes in the walls, and struck me as being distinctly unhealthy, however, "c'est la guerre," as the French say. From the top floor of this you get an astonishingly good view of the German lines, and the ground behind, and from which you send back your orders to the battery by telephone. It is the last house towards the Germans and just at a cross roads. After that we came back to the battery position, and that night about 10 o'clock my battery came in and took up its position, and I turned into my dug-out absolutely dead beat.

September 10th, 2015: Billy to Meg

My heart is now permanently in my mouth, and I leave out the pit of my tummy every morning to be cleaned with my boots. Yesterday I woke at 6.30 and got up and dressed just in time for what is known as the "morning hate." At about 8 a.m. they started on us and let us have about a dozen shells. I can hardly describe my feelings during that exceedingly "mauvais quart d'heure." They are quite indescribable, in fact. First there's a noise like a traction engine hurtling through the air at 100 miles an hour, then a whump, plop, bang, and a succession of screaming things whistling through the air all over the place, this has just subsided and you realise you're still alive when up comes another. Every shell yesterday hit me in every portion of my anatomy in imagination, but in reality the nearest was quite 30 yards off, if not more, however, curiously enough beyond that it had the most exhilarating effect, and I was astonished and delighted to find that outwardly I didn't show any signs of what was going on inside, also the men took it very well, but there's no denying that your first experience of "morning hate" is a bit trying to the nerves. However, my real joy was to come. At 2 p.m. I started out to the observing station, for what is known locally as the "afternoon strafe." On the way up a bullet whizzed past my ear, which frightened the life out of me, and then made me very angry. With grim determination and set teeth I climbed up to the top story and laid out my lines of fire on a brewery (absit omen) where the Huns (of course) were lurking. I ranged on this with great care and some skill, and at the ninth shot I put a lyddite[4] shell right through the roof of it - bricks, slates, dust, smoke, and bits of Germans flew up in every direction. It was without exception the finest moment of my life, a cheer went up from everybody, and I was waving my hat and dancing a reel on one of the rafters, nearly wild with joy. That'll teach them to put a bullet near me. It has changed my whole outlook on the War, which is a very curious thing. I am now enjoying myself immensely and don't care tuppence for them or their old shells. I wouldn't have missed this show for untold gold. I came back to the battery and told the gunners, who of course couldn't see what was happening in front of their gun pits. They also were full of delight, and it has put them absolutely right. It was a rather good performance, the 9th shot fired in action by a brand new battery to knock out a brewery. My one regret is that the exigencies of War compelled me to this act of frightfulness, and I'm sure Robert will agree with me, but again it's "la guerre." I have reason to believe that a proportion of the men share in this regret. Last night I went to bed happy, and this morning the "hymn of hate" passed over, and left us undisturbed, not to say unperturbed. This morning I went out again, and the blighters put a shell into the house next to us, but to show you the effect of the brewery shot, I was lighting a pipe at the time, and the match didn't even go out. It really is great fun out here, but they say it palls after a time - I have not found that so yet. This afternoon I wanted to take on one of their trenches, as I am now confident of my shooting, and as it is quite close to our own lines one has to be careful, so I went forward to a post in our front line to observe it, but the brutes cut my telephone wire with a shell, so I had to chuck it. I am having it repaired, and am going to do it to-morrow. We have had no casualties yet, but they killed and wounded a dozen men near the battery the other day, and two horses yesterday, so they keep us thinking.

September 19th, 1915: Billy to Meg

Many thanks for your letter. I received the cigarettes and tobacco all right, and was extremely pleased to see them, Irish tobacco is a bit trying, you have to put your ears back and pull like blazes to keep the beastly stuff alight. As regards the trunk… It was very funny about the police searching your house for explosives - I'm afraid my sword wouldn't do anybody much damage.

A lot has happened since I wrote to you last. Whether the authorities have been very much impressed with our shooting or not I can't say, but on Sunday last they moved us out to a new position about 1000 yards nearer the German

---

[4] The first British generation of modern high explosive shell.

trenches (on reading this over it looks as if they were not much impressed with our shooting, but I know that is not really the case, we have been moved to cover a more important part of the line). We are now in position near an old farm, and seem to be just as safe as in our old one, except that we get a lot more rifle bullets especially at night, this of course is due to the shorter range. I don't think I described our old position to you. It was dug in at the bottom of a beautiful old Chateau garden. We all lived in dug-outs, and messed in the garden summer-house. I wonder if you remember some letters in "Punch" addressed to the owner of the Chateau, well, they might have been written about my old position, statue of the Virgin and all. Our new position is, as I said, near a farm house. The men and the other officers live in dug-outs, but I personally am at present in the farm until I can get a dug-out constructed in case they start to shell us heavily. We are very comfortable and have a good room for the mess. I have no less than four observing stations, two of them in houses just behind the infantry trenches, and two up trees. For the tallest tree I have a cradle in which I am hauled up to the top by two hefty gunners. It is rather a perilous journey but you get a great view when you're up there. One of the house observing stations is an old barn up to the top of which I climb by a series of ladders and peer out through a small loop-hole in the roof. I have a speaking tube from it to the ground where my telephonists are in a very strong dug-out, and telephone my orders back to the battery, so but for my noble self, there is not much danger to anybody. About two nights after we got here we were rung up in the middle of the night to say that one of the infantry trenches was being attacked. I got out and got the men into action, and fired twelve rounds of lyddite at the trench by the map. I was a bit nervous about the shell, as of course I couldn't observe them at night, but we heard next morning that we had put six plumb into the German trench and the rest just over. The infantry were awfully pleased, and we got a good deal of kudos over the whole show. This gun we have got shoots extraordinarily accurately to the map range. Night shooting has a very pretty effect, a huge flash then a great cloud of smoke lit up for a second when the shell bursts. I shall never pay to go to fireworks again, every night here we have a wonderful pyrotechnic display, flares, star shell, and rockets go up at frequent intervals all night to see that both sides are up to no tricks.

Then during the day we get wonderful displays of flying. Two aeroplanes fighting in the air is the most exciting thing I have ever watched. One of our airmen brought down a German taube[5] the other day with a machine gun just behind our lines. It is also most amusing watching each side's anti-aircraft guns shelling the other's machines, you see the shells bursting all round them and think they must be hit. Our anti-aircraft guns are called "Archibald," they are the butt of the whole force, they have never been known to hit anything. When Archibald starts shooting you can hear ripples of laughter all along the line.

---

[5] pigeon

Yesterday I had rather a thrilling experience. I had to go and reconnoitre an advanced position just short of the German front trench, so I went down to our front trench behind which to position, but found to my intense disgust that I couldn't see what I wanted to from the trench, so there was nothing for it but to climb out behind, and run about 100 yards in the open to the shelter of a haystack where I could see what I wanted. Talk about the game of "lines," you should have seen me run that 100, the world's record was easily eclipsed. I think the Boches were so surprised that they didn't shoot till too late, anyhow they didn't get one near me. It's extraordinary how one can get used to anything, we get shelled regularly twice a day and nobody turns a hair, and as for rifle bullets you hardly notice them. Another great point about War is the wonderful cheeriness of everyone. One seems to be perpetually laughing at things that in normal times would make your hair stand on end. All the ordinary trifling worries of life seem to be relegated to oblivion, as long as you're alive at the end of the day nothing seems to matter a bit. I don't know when I've laughed so heartily as at -----[6] when I was out with him the other day. We were about 100 yards apart looking at some telephone wires when a shell burst just behind him. He went down like a shot rabbit and I thought for a moment that he had been hit, then I saw a very pale face rising gingerly up behind a tuft of grass, and a very shaky voice said "Good Lord, old man, did you see that?" I was immediately convulsed with laughter, and he was quite stuffy about it. The men are very cheerful, cracking jokes the whole time; during the night firing one of them kept saying as he jerked the handle, "That'll teach the brutes to get me out of bed at this time of night" – only he didn't say brutes. I was talking to a private in the Leinsters down in the trenches the other day, a Kildare man, and he was very anxious to know when I thought the War would be over (the infantry soldier always ascribes an omniscience to Artillery officers that they are far from possessing). So to cheer him up and encourage him to further efforts I said that it was only a question of killing enough of them, and they wouldn't be able to go on for want of men. "Where do you think," said I, "that they'll get the men from to replace their losses?" "Begob, sir," said he, "they hatch thim in the thrinches, for ivery wan ye'd kill there does be two in his place."

One of the most interesting things in this War is the getting to know the habits of the enemy, who's shooting at you (I mean guns, of course,) and where they are, and devising all sorts of schemes to outwit them. One favourite is to lull somebody you've marked down into a false sense of security by shooting about 40 degrees away from him, then suddenly switching your guns round, and letting him have a burst of rapid fire before he has time to go to ground, but it's very hard to defeat the wily Hun. By some extraordinary telepathy it has grown up that the Artillery knock off between 1 and 2 for lunch; this is an absolute rule, and if either side by any chance violate it the others give them a great lambasting about

---

[6] censored

5 p.m. to make up for it. So that if we hear a gun fired by our side at 1.10 we know we may look out for trouble that afternoon, on the other hand if a shell drops on our lines between 1 and 2 we arrange a great "strafe" for a certain hour and let them have it back 100 fold. It's wonderful what a salutary effect it has, you can almost always count on a peaceful lunch.

We are also getting to know the German battery commanders' tricks quite well, in fact we are on Christian name terms. One frequently gets rung up on the telephone by a message like this – "That blighter Oscar fired at me this morning when I was writing home, give him Hell, will you, old boy." So you at once lay out your lines on Oscar's battery, and duly proceed to give him hell. There is really, in a sense, quite a feeling of friendliness towards the enemy. There was one important spot in our lines, and we were ordered if ever the Germans shelled it, to send back two for every one of theirs, after about four days of this they chucked it. What really annoys the Hun, however, is when you drop a shell in his infantry trenches - he can't stand that. It's great fun doing this - like stirring a wasps' nest with a stick. I am enjoying myself immensely, I didn't believe one really could have enjoyed War so much, it is full of incident, and something fresh to look forward to every day. The feeling that you don't know what moment will be your next, so to speak, has a most exhilarating effect, and keeps you from a single moment's boredom. I hope you are all going strong at home. I heard from Rowan, and am writing to him.

September 20th, 1915: Billy to Thornley

Many thanks for your letter. Of course you may use my sword, I wrote to your Mother and Molly to this effect some time ago. I hope you'll get your Commission in the R.F.A., there is no doubt the gunners have all the fun in this War at present. The infantry in the trenches daren't put their heads up except at night, so they see very little, but we crawl to our observing stations, and then climb up into roofs, trees, chimneys, steeples etc., and have a great view until we're spotted, and then it is healthier to seek a more salubrious spot. It is rather like a glorified game of tennis, with the Artillery as the players and the trenches as the net, with this difference that one into the net counts for you instead of against you, but an odd lob on the back line, or even out, is sometimes wonderfully efficacious. It is most glorious fun, and beats shooting, hunting, and fishing all rolled into one. A great point about being a battery commander is that you have so much to think about and attend to that you have no time to feel frightened. Even when you are being shelled, and are not replying, which is the most trying experience, you've generally got your brain hard at work devising some means of getting your own back. The men are pretty safe in their dug-outs, everyone is pleased. We have all sorts of methods of hoodwinking the Hun, which may be useful to you. As I daresay you know, it is almost, in fact absolutely, impossible, to see a battery in this sort of warfare; any battery that could be seen direct would be finished in ten minutes, because every gun anywhere near would turn on to it; consequently they are all perfectly concealed from view by earth emplacements carefully sodded over and planted with oats or bushes etc., which merge with the background. For instance, I am dug in on the edge of a cornfield, so my dug-outs are planted with oats, which will be reaped and made into stooks at the proper season. It follows therefore that your only chance to hit the other fellow is to get his locality as near as possible by sound or flash, or by seeing his men moving about, and then to plaster all that area with shell in the hope of a few catching him. The tip is, when you are firing and the other fellow is searching for you, when he reaches a point well away from you, stop firing at once. He then pats himself on the back and says "I've silenced him, anyway," and 10-1 if you start firing again the next day he will open on the spot where he thought he silenced you the day before. On the other hand, if he gets one in, fire as hard as you can, and he will probably switch to another part, thinking he is nowhere near you. To hoodwink him still further it is well enough to reverse this process at odd periods. That is, for 3 days go on as above, and then for the next 4 do the exact opposite. This will keep him thinking. Another good dodge is to fire at night, and as each gun is fired have a very obvious flash let off about 300 yards to your flank. I couldn't tell you all the tricks of the trade in one letter, but I will try and keep you posted from time to time. The thing you must learn and make yourself absolutely proficient in is taking ranges and angles quickly and accurately from a map. I have done every bit of my shooting from the map since I have been here, with some success. One never uses a director or plotter. I hope failing the Commn. you will get the Junr. Ex., but you get out here as quickly as you can if you want to enjoy yourself.

September 29th, 1915: Billy to Meg

I am afraid I haven't written to you for a long time, but I literally have not had a moment. In these strenuous times you must not mind or be anxious if I do not write for some time, as a Battery Commander's work leaves him with very little leisure. I received the cake, in splendid condition, the collars, the piece of soap, maple sugar and a box of matches, for all of which many thanks. The cake was much appreciated by the mess and the other things are most useful. I also received another consignment of cigarettes and tobacco from Mitchell's.

And now for my news. As you will have gathered, when I wrote last we were merely engaged in siege warfare, and enjoying it immensely, a friendly interchange of shots, regular meals etc., but of course we were preparing for this big battle[7] though I couldn't tell you, and for the last ten days we have been fairly in the thick of it. I suppose it is the biggest battle in the world's history. I had no conception of what war was really like before, and my views have undergone another violent change. It is horrible, there is no other word for it. I have had a most awful shock, and have seen sights that are far too terrible for words; however, I will try and tell you in chronological order.

---

[7] Battle of Loos

Some time ago we had all received our secret orders for this show, and the whole thing was cut and dried except the day and time of commencement which was kept secret up till the last minute. On Monday 20th we were sent for to Headquarters and told that the battle has been settled to begin at 4.25 the next morning, the prelude was a four days' Artillery bombardment, and then on the 5th day the attack. So on Tuesday[8] at 4.25 the show began. I have never heard such a terrific row in the whole course of my life, it was like Hell let loose. All day the Artillery bombarded, though of course my battery weren't firing all day, and at intervals during the night. This went on for four solid days and nights, and what with our guns and the Germans replying, my head was bazzing round, and my nerves were all on edge, it was like a nightmare. On Sat. 25th, the infantry assault was timed for 4.30 a.m., and for five minutes before it every gun from Switzerland to the sea was firing as hard as it could. I, of course, was up at my observing station, and it was the most wonderful sight. It was pitch dark when we started, and the flashes of the guns and then the flashes of the bursting shells split the darkness like lightning, the din was indescribable. Nothing could have lived in the fire we poured on the German trenches, and five minutes later when the infantry charged, they simply walked through, there was nothing against them. We, of course, meantime had lengthened our range and were firing over their heads. By 6 a.m. we had captured the front enemy trench all along the line, the infantry then went on to the second and third line trenches, where they met with a good deal more opposition, especially from machine guns, and then they would send back to us, and we would switch our fire on to the places they indicated wanted knocking out, all went well up to 1 p.m., we had got the third line in most places and were consolidating our position.

There was an advanced dressing station just beside my observing station, and from time to time I would go down and hear from the wounded how the attack was progressing. Curiously enough, the first wounded officer I saw was Edward French of the Lincolns, who had been hit in the arm by a Maxim. He is probably in Dublin by this time. I had a talk with him, he seemed quite cheery and I don't think his wound was serious. He is a brother of Michael French, Robert's friend. It was a horrible sight when the more serious cases began to be brought in, but they were all very cheerful, and a lot of them were wearing German helmets, of which they were exceedingly proud. However, I had to go down there as I was getting a lot of useful information from them; a lot of the Royal Irish Rifles were brought in there. The worst of the thing was that the Germans were shelling it the whole time, and they had to take the ones that couldn't be got away quickly to the cellars. To resume, at 1 p.m. the Germans started their counter-attack, supported by a tremendous Artillery fire. I saw masses of them moving down from the reserves, and was just getting into them nicely when they got the range of my battery and subjected it to a terrific cannonade. The men were splendid,

---

[8] 21 September 1915

and went on firing as coolly as possible, but I regret to say that the Huns put a shell, a direct hit, on my no. 1 gun, and knocked it out, killing the whole detachment of five men. We carried on with three guns, and then they put a shell into my telephone dug-out, killing one signaller and wounding three others. It was now obvious that they had got the range exactly, I think as a fact we were given away by an aeroplane or a spy, so to avoid further loss of life the men were withdrawn to some trenches on a flank. The Germans continued their fire, but did no further damage so when it had slackened a bit I took the men back and withdrew the three remaining guns to another position, we had a driver wounded getting them away, but that was all our casualties for that day. That night we dug all night putting the guns in their new position, and next day I had to go back with my sergt-major and two sergts (I didn't want the young fellows to be unnerved by any gruesome sights) to get out the remaining gun, and the bodies of the gun detachment. The shell had come through the roof of the gun-emplacement and burst inside, smashing the gun up, and mangling fearfully the men inside. The roof had fallen in on them, and we had to dig them out.

Mercifully, death was instantaneous in all cases – I don't suppose any of them knew they were hit. I will spare you any further details, but it gave me an awful shock, it took us all day to get them out, and several tots of rum to keep us going. The horrors of war is no idle expression. To add to our difficulties, a whole lot of live ammunition was buried with the gun, so we had to be very careful. The wounded, I am glad to say, are all doing well. We are now all completely recovered, and very happy again. The men were again splendid, and though they all got a fearful shock, pulled themselves together wonderfully next day, and are now going strong, and longing for a chance to get their own back. We won a great victory, and have gained a lot of ground. The French down south of us we hear are doing splendidly, and have taken over 1800 prisoners, so I think there ought to be a general advance before the winter, but it is very hard to look at these things in their proper proportions.

The next night I was half dead with fatigue, I was badly shaken up, and felt more as if we had suffered a defeat than gained a victory. However it's extraordinary how soon one recovers out here. All are as cheery as possible now, but I have had a tremendous amount of work getting into the new position, arranging the burials, settling up the affairs of the men. I am also writing to each man's next of kin. They were splendid fellows and some of my best gunners. I lost altogether a Sergt, a Bombr, and four gunners killed, a Corpl and three men wounded. It hits the battery very hard. The gun I hope to have replaced in a day or two. We had to bury the men that night in a cemetery behind our front lines, and we were being sniped at by Germans the whole time, which is a dirty trick, though I don't suppose they knew what we were at. We are all in great hope of driving these brutes out of France before the winter, but I'm afraid all the fun has gone out of it now, it's serious business. It has lost all its sporting side. They are using gas shells again, and every device they can think of, and all the prisoners we take seem to be heartily sick of the whole show.

My new position is an excellent one, I hope they won't find it again, but these aeroplanes are the very devil, usually one stops firing when they are overhead, but of course in battle one can't. We have been very quiet on this part of the line to-day, hardly a shot been fired. I don't know what's up, but I mistrust the wily Hun even when not sending shells; he is probably trying to lull us into a false sense of security. I hope you are all going strong at home, and that the news is cheering, it's very hard to find out what's happening here except on your immediate front. You might let Rowan know what's in my letters, as I have not time to write so much to everyone.

October 2nd, 1915: Rowan's first letter to Meg

I am at a reinforcement camp in France, where I expect to stay a few days before joining the battalion. Pearson and Gomme of ours came with me.

We got to London on the evening of the 30th, where as an old campaigner I decided that the instructions "to proceed to Folkstone as quickly as possible," would be sufficiently complied with if we had a comfortable night, and a little shopping the next morning. We arrived at the embarkation office at 3 o'clock, where we were informed that a boat left in half an hour. Going on board we found officers from other Whitchurch regiments[9], who had travelled the whole night, and kicked their heels about Folkstone all day. They were awfully sick when they heard of our pleasant and leisurely progress.

We arrived here about 10.30 p.m. yesterday evening with about a dozen others were conducted to empty tents with no lights. After a short look I segregated my two comrades, and we walked into the town, and had a comfortable night in a hostel. We arrived in camp in time to report at 9 o'clock this morning, and found the others very grumpy after an uncomfortable night on beds laid down in the dark. I impressed upon them that common sense was a large element in the art of war, which they did not seem to like.

I am very glad to be here in the middle of things. The weather is good, and I am feeling very fit.

October 4th, 1915: Rowan to Meg

We have been summoned up to join the 9th Cheshires, the old battalion, to-day. We start in ten minutes. Have no time to write more at present so au revoir.

---

[9] The 9th (Service) Battalion, Cheshire Regiment was billeted in the Basingstoke area over the winter of 1914.

October 6th, 1915: Rowan to Meg

I am now at the side of the road near our Divisional Headquarters with five other officers of the Division, waiting for our kits to be transported to our Billets. We have had an interesting journey since we left for the front on Monday afternoon, as we have been passing long a line about 5-7 miles behind the firing line. The guns have been firing ceaselessly, and their flashes and that of the flares have illumined the night. We started very comfortably in first class carriages, but were soon shifted into baggage trucks, and have been sleeping on railway platforms etc. On Monday night we boarded the Transport Officer's train, which looked comfortable, and were just making ourselves comfortable when the latter turned up, and just refrained from putting a revolver bullet through me. He was a very nervy person, and had shot a man in similar circumstances the previous night.

This morning we were put on a motor lorry, and driven here. We found that our brigade had been detached, but is expected back to-morrow, when we shall join it.

I met Cowdy's brother[10] in the boat, who was going to drive a Red Cross motor, and a man called McIntyre from Dublin in the R.A.M.C.[11], with whom I had been at T.C.D., turned up at our base the other day. The places out here are all very damp. I am feeling very fit.

October 6th, 1915: Billy to Meg

I received all your parcels and letters…

As you have no doubt guessed, since I wrote to you last we have moved again forward, and have had to dig ourselves in all over again. The poor part of this new position is that there is no farm building or building of any sort to live in, everything here is in ruins, so for the last week we have been living in what I can only describe as a wet ditch. However, I have now constructed a dug-out for myself in which I am writing this, and it is fairly comfortable. We have also managed to secure an empty tool-shed for a mess, so we are not too badly off.

A lull has come in the great battle, and we are enjoying a period of comparative quiet which is very welcome. Everybody is as cheery as possible, and only waiting for the word to go in and finish them off. I have found an excellent observation station quite close up to our new trench where I can see splendidly. I sat and watched four Boches yesterday improving their dug-outs, and I could distinguish their features quite clearly.

There was a very funny incident the day before; a German officer, a very gallant fellow, climbed out of his trench, stood up on the parapet, and fired three shots from a rifle into our trenches, he then got down, walked away and in a little while came back, climbed up again and set down on the parapet and smoked a

---

[10] Harry Cowdy was Rowan's partner in his law practice in Malasia.
[11] Royal Artillery Medical Corps.

cigarette, the while he shook his fist in our direction and was obviously cursing us. Nobody took the slightest notice of him, or fired a shot at him. I don't know what he was after, I think he must have been tired of life in the trenches or perhaps he had got into trouble and wanted to commit suicide. He was obviously very much disgusted when none of our fellows obliged him with a bullet. As a fact, I don't think any of the infantry saw him.

We got a lot of kudos for the battle, and received the thanks of two generals for our services. The Corps Commander came and inspected us and gave them to us personally, and the other one mentioned us in his orders. Thank you very much for your congratulations on my promotion. The first thing I heard of it was a telephone message from the Colonel congratulating me, and during the morning the General came down and said: "Good morning, Major Shaw, merit rewarded at last, eh?" which was very nice of him and very pleasing to me. We have got an extraordinarily nice lot of senior people over us and I get on splendidly with them all. The funniest thing of all was the men, they were very different at first as to whether it was correct discipline to congratulate their C.O.; however, they finally plucked up courage and filed into my dug-out singly, came smartly to attention, and made a little set speech, some of their remarks being too funny for words; at the end of this levee, however, I was nearer tears than laughter. They are splendid fellows, and I have forwarded the names of four of them for steadiness under fire during the great "strafe." The chief difference my promotion makes is in the matter of pay, as I have the same command as a Major that I had as a Captain, at which I am extremely pleased, as I would hate to hand this battery over to anyone else now. It is the most delightful command anyone could have, and I have made it all myself from the very beginning. As you know, when I formed it last December they were just a collection of men thrown together, no N.C.O.s, horses, guns, or anything, and now they are a first-class battery that have come through a very trying ordeal with flying colours. All this, as you can imagine, is very gratifying to me, because there must always be a certain amount of doubt in everyone's mind as to whether the thing he has fashioned will stand the test of practical experience. I have now absolute confidence in them, and I think they have confidence in me. It's really great luck for me, as very few men have had the chance of taking a battery they've formed themselves on service.

We have had a very fine variety of weathers here since I wrote to you, wet, cold, fine and warm. To-day is a very fine mellow autumn day, with a lot of warmth in the sun, but it gets very chilly towards evening. There has hardly been a shot fired all day on either side. I have a good position here which I hope they don't discover. We had a bullet through the top of the tool-shed the other night while we were at dinner, and another one has just dropped outside the palatial abode, but these are merely incidents, – probably badly aimed stray ones. It would be rotten luck to be knocked out by a bad shot!

There's no doubt now in my mind that these Germans are swine. They were seen by a British officer in the battle putting a lot of our wounded into a trench and bombing them to death; also just in front of my observation station there are a lot of British corpses lying in the No Man's Land between the two front trenches, but almost against the German parapet. The brutes are making no effort to bury them, which of course they could easily do at night. Of course it's quite impossible for our fellows to get near them as the Huns would shoot them down if they tried, whereas we would gladly let them bury them.

I heard from Rowan just a line to say he had got his orders to start, please let me know as soon as you hear where he has gone to, and what Battn. You were not quite right about the Battle. The bombardment only lasted four days, and then the fifth day the great "Strafe," and on the night of the sixth day I got into bed, so I didn't have to go without sleep for ten days. I think all the sleep I have been saving up in my youth must be standing to me now, as I didn't seem to miss it until I had finally finished off everything, then I was ready to drop.

I was awfully glad to hear about Thornley's commission, Exeter is a jolly place. Tell him to let me know all about who his seniors are, I am certain to know some of them and may be able to help him. I wonder when he'll get out here, it would be splendid if I could get him into this Division, but I don't suppose they'll send him for at least six months, and by that time, please God, we'll have them fairly on the run. You are now in the proud position of being sister to one of the youngest Majors, and mother to one of the youngest Sec-Lts in the British Army, not to mention being sister to one of the oldest Sec-Lts – ha, ha, poor old Rowan!

Give my love to all at 39, also the pup to whom you might give a bone with my love. I expect the little devil has forgotten me by now.

October 7th, 1915: Rowan to Meg

Have just rejoined B Coy. 9th Cheshire Regt., my old Coy. They have just returned from six weeks in the trenches. I am taking two platoons out to bathe, and will write later. A cake or two for our mess would be grateful and comforting.

October 10th, 1915: Billy to Robert

There has been a lull for the last week on this part of the front, and we are enjoying a life of comparative peace again, back to the old siege warfare, which I enjoy tremendously, and is most amusing. Battles are most unpleasant things, and if we have many more of them your trade[12] will be booming, I wonder I have any drums left at all. We have taken up an entirely new position, and I have had to design and construct myself a dug-out which, though I say it who shouldn't, is a master-piece. Its interior is 15ft. By 9, it is 6 ft. deep at the shallow end and about 8 ft. at the other. It is lined with planks with a 6 in. air space between the walls

---

[12] surgeon

and the earth, and similarly has a wood floor raised 6 in., the walls are covered with brown Holland, and I have looted an oil stove to heat it. The bed is made of canvas stretched on a wood frame work and raised on four legs, very comfortable. The wash-stand is an old French churn standing on end, and I have looted 2 tables, 2 chairs, a mirror, an oak chest, a lamp and a candlestick. I am now keeping a weather eye open for a carpet to complete my comfort. It is roofed with sheets of corrugated iron, covered with earth, then three feet of sandbags, then a layer of bricks sodded all over to merge with the ground. The only thing is that everybody says that by the beginning of December we will be flooded out, the country is low-lying, and as soon as the numerous rivers and streams begin to rise we won't be able to live in dug-outs, so I am now devising a scheme to drain the water into a big hole and pump it out every day.

There is one thing I want you to make a note of, i.e., my servant and my groom (Br. Roberts and Gr. Barfield) want me to save up their wages for them until the end of the war, then give them a lump sum. They are paid at the rate of 10/- a month, so that if anything happens to me I owe them whatever sum has accrued at this rate from September 1st, 1915. I should also like Br. H. Roberts, my servant, to have £100, and my groom, Gr. Barfield to have £50, out of my estate in a like eventuality, there ought to be a sufficient sum to my credit at Cox's to pay this. I am now drawing roughly £35 a month and hardly spending anything except the various things, tobacco etc. I am getting from home, so my credit will be going up by leaps and bounds. It is the first time in my life that I consider that my services have met with an adequate pecuniary recognition.

I was awfully glad to hear that Thornley had got his commission, I should think he will make an excellent Artillery officer. I daresay we'll have Jack in the thick of it before we succeed in finishing these blighters off. They're horrible brutes, but they're certainly wonderfully efficient soldiers, at least their officers know their job from A to Z, but I don't think the private is a patch on ours, they surrendered in shoals the other day, poor old men in spectacles and young boys. Once the iron hand of immediate personal supervision (pardon the mixture of metaphors) is off them, they are useless. Whereas our fellows go on just as well when the wily Hun comes in, because our officers lead their men into action, and of course are outed first and sacrifice themselves, the Bosch, like the celebrated Duke of Plaza Toro[13], lead their regiments from behind with a revolver in one hand, and as they are pretty good shots, their wretched men think they might as well be shot by us and be covered in glory, as be shot by their own covers and be covered with infamy. Consequent on all this, it is very hard for us to kill, wound, or capture anything like the proper proportion of German officers, who clear out when things are going badly, go and collect another batch of cannon fodder, and drive them into the forefront of the battle again. "C'est la guerre, mais ce n'est

---

[13] Gilbert & Sullivan *The Gondoliers*

pas magnifique."[14] Our shortage of officers at the present rate will be appalling at the end of another year. We lost two Divisional Generals in this last show, an unheard of thing in most wars.

The Balkan situation looks serious, I wonder if Greece is really going to rat. I can't imagine where we're going to raise another Expeditionary Force. One thing is, the Regular survivors ought all to be Colonels at least before it's over. "It's an ill wind etc." I hope you are all going strong at home as this leaves me, I haven't heard a word about Rowan, but I suppose that will come along in due course. Tell Megsie I received the letter-pad for which many thanks.

October 10th, 1915: Rowan to Meg

Thanks for your letter of Oct 6th. The parcel you mention has not rolled up yet, but will no doubt arrive in due course. I also have received the various copies of Billy's letters which are most interesting reading. I'm afraid the experiences of a "foot-slogger" like myself will not be anything like so piquant. The life out here is very interesting. We live in the farm-buildings and cottages; there are no Chateaux in this neighbourhood. The men live in barns. Three of us sleep in a small room at the end of a cottage, and we have our company mess of four in the kitchen of another cottage. The men are in the outbuildings all round, and the cottagers and their friends and refugees are all round us. The French are very kind and hospitable, but a bit "on the make." I find my bit of French very useful, and it is coming back, but the Malay word still presents itself first. The regiment is just back from the trenches, where the Brigade was in the recent attack. The casualties were heavy, officers and men, but all behaved splendidly. We shall probably be in it again in a few days. They were five weeks in the trenches last time, but I think this is exceptional. One of ours, one E. Watts Sec-Lieut, who has been wounded is at 33 Upper Fitzwilliam St. You might look him up and see if you can do anything for him. He is a very decent chap.

October 11th, 1915: Rowan to Meg,

Many thanks for parcel received. Every item was of the most useful description. I have got my clothing washed here, so you need not send any clothes until you hear further. I led two platoons out for a hot bath in a brewery the other day. It was their first bath for three months, and mine for a week, so we fairly solidified the water. I have fairly settled down now, and am in charge of my old platoon in my old company, which is very pleasant. Life at the front so far as I have had the opportunity of observing it, is very pleasant indeed. We mess in companies, and there are four of us in B Coy. They are all charming people whom I like very much, and we live very happily together. I hope I shall not be shifted to C who have only two officers left. The regiment is in very good spirits in spite of heavy

---

[14] Gen. Pierre Bosquet: *"C'est magnifique, mais ce n'est pas la guerre: c'est de la folie."*

losses, and the brigade, the 58th Infantry, have received special commendation from the Corps Commander. One of the Welsh regiments brigaded with us started the attack in a most sportive spirit. An officer "punted" a football, with the names of the four platoons on it over the parapet, shouted "Follow up, boys," and jumped over the parapet followed by the whole platoon. They opened the machine guns immediately and he fell back into the trench shot through the heart. Our brigade did not gain much ground, as the enemy's machine gun had not been properly knocked out.

We had a festive dinner with A Coy in their cottage on Saturday night, and are returning their hospitality to-morrow night, it being Jackson's (the Captain's) birthday. The chickens are the main delicacy 11lbs of hen costing 13 francs. The champagne is cheap but I do not know if it will be much good.

Censoring the men's letters is amusing at first; one of my blackguards, with an eye no doubt to the future, wrote to his best girl that – "one of our old officers, Mr. Shaw, has returned, he has shaved his upper lip, and looks in the pink of condition." I had no sooner got back than a hint was conveyed within three days. If you go to see Watts, tell him I have taken over his platoon and his stick, and will look after both well. We expect to go back to the trenches this week.

Glad to hear from Molly that you are having a run to Belfast, I am sure it will do you good. Have just noticed your note in letter pad. I shall be delighted to lend my camp kit to Thornley. He will want a canvas bucket and basin, which I have here. Give him my congratulations on his Commission.

October 15th, 1915: Billy to Molly

Blessings on you for all your letters, which I am afraid I have been very remiss in answering, but I find when I get a long one off to your mother, all my available time has been used up. It was very good of you to write to me so soon after your arrival in Cambridge. I hope you will enjoy yourself there. I should think it ought to be great fun for you, that is if they don't make you work too hard, but I suppose they are stuffing your head with all sorts of knowledge. Always remember that it is of more educational value to know the principle of the common pump than Keats' Ode to a Grecian Urn. This Obiter Dicta is very well exemplified out here, where as you may imagine the aforesaid Ode, whatever its aesthetic value, would be of no practical use, whereas the knowledge of the innards of the pump makes all the difference between sleeping dry and warm or in a perpetual cold bath. Considering all things, however, we are keeping wonderfully cheerful. My chief amusement when I'm not shooting is to wander down to our new trench, of which we are all very proud, and listen to our Tommies chaffing the Bosches over the way. "Hi, Fritz, 'am and heggs for von" always brings a response of a volley of bullets. It is very easy to pull a Hun's leg, I'm afraid they have a very limited sense of humour. They threw a lot of notes over the other night, saying, "You can have these trenches on the 14th, we're off" – but they show no signs of moving yet, I expect it only meant that they were to be relieved by another regiment. We have had several very high compliments paid us in documents captured on German prisoners, in which the German General Staff is very frank in explaining to the solders how they can best deal with us. To quote only one - "The enemies' Artillery is very accurate, and their observation is excellent, but we cannot discover whether this is carried out from the air or from observation posts on the ground. It is the duty of every soldier to endeavour to locate these posts and report them at once" – how's that for a pat on the back from the hated enemy? It is more cheering to read a sentence like that than volumes of praise from our own side. Rowan is out here now, and I am trying to discover where he is to see if I could arrange to meet him on an off day. When Thornley comes out, the family will be fairly doing its bit. Cheeroh!

October 15th, 1915: Billy to Bobby

Many thanks for your letter. I determined not to answer it until I had been in a real battle. Well, I have been in one now, and I don't mind confessing to you, as a man of the world, that I wouldn't break my heart if I never was in another. They are nasty damned miserable unpleasant things, and make your head ache for about a fortnight after them. I hope you are following your uncle's excellent example in sticking closely to your studies… Boys who have learnt first to obey and then to command, to pull together and play the game, are now the men that are contributing largely to the arduous task of wiping these blighted Huns off the face of the earth. I'm sure it is quite unnecessary for me to tell you not to neglect the athletic side of your school life, it keeps you fit, happy, and out of mischief. The saying that "Waterloo was won on the playing fields of Eton" is no less true to-day than it was 100 years ago, or than it will be 20 or 100 years hence.

We are having a period of comparative peace here at present, and are just sitting here potting a shell or two now and then. We hope to be let loose at them again before long, we have got an old score to settle with them now, and the men are all straining at the leash to be into them once more. The weather is fine but dull. I have built myself a sumptuous dug-out here which is the envy of the whole of Northern France, luxuriously furnished in the style of the Oct. 1915 period, chiefly loot, and guaranteed damp proof, but not to any specified extent. My chief amusement when I get a few spare hours is to go down to our new forward trench, and listen to our men chaffing the Bosches over the way.

The other afternoon I was there and remarked to a little Cockney friend of mine in one of the London Regts, that it seemed pretty quiet. "I'll soon wake them up for you, sir," says he, and seizing a megaphone, he shouted, "'Ullo, there, Fritz, 'ave you run hout of ammunition this afternoon or wot?" - This was immediately followed by a terrific fusillade of bullets from the Huns. We sat under the parapet full of joy at the waste of ammunition. It's very easy to pull their legs. "Hi, Fritz, 'am and heggs for von"- always produces a rise. Tommy is under the firm conviction that every German alive is, has been or will be a waiter, and I'm not sure that he's far wrong.

Give my love to Johnny, and tell him that if he doesn't write to me soon, it'll be two with the back, and two with the bristles when I get home.

October 22nd, 1915: Thornley to Molly

My dear Molly,

Thank you so much for your letter which I received just before parting with my friends at Shrewsbury. I own that I should have answered before but I have been rather busy settling in here and getting the hang of things generally.

This is really, for a barracks, a top hole place but there is not much to do when you are off parade. Almost all the men here are colonials and their interests and sympathies are so different from mine that it is almost impossible to find a common meeting ground, still they are very good fellows and we get on well enough.

I went down to the town this afternoon after a very strenuous morning first at riding then at gun drill and then at stable inspection. I was introduced to the Colonel who seems a kindly old bird and am thinking of calling on him this afternoon.

While down town I got a chance to see the cathedral, after walking round I decided that it was very nice, it is all the same style, late Gothic except the south transept and I believe that the choir is later. I did not go in because they were having a service and I had neither the time nor the inclination.

Your affectionate and ever loving brother, Thornley

October 22nd, 1915: Billy to Meg

The old grey horse was awfully ashamed of himself the day he was dyed, the mare didn't recognise him, and tried to kick him out of his own stall (they had been the best of friends previously), and for a week he went about hanging his head and with a listless gait, but he has got used to it now and has perked up again.

I was very much interested and amused by the doings of the pup; I am beginning to lose hope of ever getting him back now without bringing you into court, and even then I doubt if he'd want to come. He had the most marvelous knack of endearing himself to everybody with whom he comes into contact, it was the same wherever I went in England. There was a certain Major, a most inveterate dog-hater, in the Mess at Chester, who at first tried hard to get me forbidden to keep him in barracks – needless to say without success – and who after about a month used to be very sick if I didn't bring Mick in to tea in the anteroom. When this cruel war is o'er if I can't get Mick back, I shall get another of his small relatives from Flood[15]; I don't think I would like any other breed now.

It must have been a great wrench for you parting with Thornley, but he'll probably be able to get several whacks of leave home before long. I don't suppose they'll send him out here for a long time yet. If and when they do, I will do my utmost to get him appointed to this Division and will then be able to keep an avuncular eye on him. I am expecting a letter from him from Exeter before long. Molly wrote to me from Cambridge, and seems to be enjoying herself; she had joined the local Fire Brigade, if I read her correctly.

I have written to Rowan and am trying to arrange to meet him if possible. We are a bit north of the place you mention, but I think I can manage to get a lift in a motor someday, and go down and see him.

Things have been fairly peaceful here lately except for an occasional little scrap, we haven't yet quite settled on the ownership of the "Hohenzollern" redoubt[16], which is about the only cause for excitement at present. The weather has been very foggy, so the Artillery have not had much opportunity of doing their usual good work. It looks very much, I'm afraid, as if we had settled down for another winter. I was full of hope, at one time, that we were going to get them really on the move before the winter, but now I'm afraid not. We have the divil of a tough job in front of us if we're going to break through on this front. We can see from here with a telescope another line, or series of lines of entrenchments right back, and Lord knows how many more there are that we can't see. I am enclosing you an extract from a German's diary which will amuse you, which was captured by the French.

1. "Lieutenant Reinacker is drunk…"
2. "Lieutenant Reinacker is drunk…"
3. "This evening our Lt. Reinacker went sick…"
4. "To-day we made an attack…Lt. Reinacker could be heard ceaselessly shouting 'Vorwarts' from the second line dugouts…"
5. "Our Lieutenant Reinacker has been awarded the Iron Cross."

This will serve to show you the type of blighter we are up against here. How these German officers get their men to do anything for them beats me. They must have a discipline of which we have no conception.

I get a certain amount of fun out of going down to the front line trench and hearing the Tommies chipping the Huns over the way. The cockney beats everyone else hollow at this game, I suppose because he has a more intimate acquaintance with them than anyone else, but the astonishing thing is the fluency of the idiomatic English in which they reply, which I won't soil my ears by repeating. The cockney has a firm conviction, which nothing will eradicate, that

---

[15] Flood was the lion keeper at the Dublin Zoo.
[16] The Hohenzollern Redoubt was fought over from the battle of Loos in October 1915 to the battle of the Somme in July 1916.

every German is a waiter, either actual or potential, and consequently to pull their legs he keeps shouting orders for various dishes or pots of beer, which naturally enough annoys the Huns exceedingly. A demand for sausages nearly always brings a replay of a hail of bullets, this is followed by a criticism in no measured terms of the quality of the sausages supplied, and a threat that if they don't improve he'll get the sack, or words to that effect, this with any luck will bring a trench mortar shell, which is then marked down, telephoned back to the guns, who proceed to knock it out. It's quite a good game, and helps to pass what would otherwise be a rather dull time.

Please don't think that your home chatter bores me, or anything like that, it's most refreshing to read of all your doings at home – in fact, creates an atmosphere, which is the art of all great writers. I have had a most interesting correspondence with Sir Gilbert Parker, the novelist, which I will tell you about anon.

Tell Robert that I thought his portrait of you excellent, and that I am looking forward to receiving the pair of socks he knitted. We wear very big boots out here. Please convey my best thanks to Patsy for her very interesting letter, which I will answer in due course.

October 25th, 1915: Billy to Patricia

Many thanks for your most interesting letter, which achieved what Sam Weller[17] described as the highest art in letter-writing, namely to make the recipient "vish there vos more of it." This is only my little joke, and I think for a child of your age[18] it was a most creditable performance. I am answering it on the Active Service Compendium which you so kindly gave me last Christmas. I have a dim recollection of saying at the time that I never had received a more useful collection of presents, and to show that I was not only just saying things after the fashion of grown-ups, I have at present in use out here Mother's cigarette lighter, Molly's handkerchiefs, Thornley's knife, Jack's book, and your letter-case, as you will see by this, the first letter written in it. Daddy's cigars and Bobby's shaving-soap having done their duty nobly, have long since gone the way – well, the way of all cigars and shaving-soap.

We are having a very quiet time out here at present, in fact almost inclined to be dull, but nevertheless it has its humours, if one has the knack of looking at things in that light. Not long ago when things were more exciting, I was watching a small boy, not much older than you, ploughing a field close behind where my battery was in action. He was sitting on his plough driving the horse, serenely unconscious of all danger. Presently shells began to fall around the battery, and about ten minutes later one dropped in the field about 20 yards from this small boy. I was not surprised to see him nip off his plough pretty quick, but to my

---

[17] Dickens *The Pickwick Papers*.
[18] 11 years

intense astonishment and amusement instead of running away he ran as fast as he could to the shell-hole and dived down it like a rabbit. When I had recovered from my surprise, I went over and seized a bare leg which was all I could see, and hauled him to the surface. He then explained to me with a grin all over his face, that he wanted the fuse for a souvenir. Luckily the shell was blind, that is, did not explode, or he would have been blown to pieces. He seemed very much aggrieved, when, in the best French I could muster, I read him a lecture on not meddling with things he did not understand, and sent him home, plough and all, to his mother. The peasants here are astonishing, they literally have no fear. One family, when I went to see if any of them were alive after their house had been hit by a shell a minute before, received me with smiles, and pointed out what rotten shots the Bosches were, as they had not even stopped the clock.

I have at present on my table in front of me, letters from Molly, Thornley, Jack, Bobby, and yourself, which must constitute a record, four of them from different parts of the United Kingdom. I hope you are all going strong and well, and that the pup and Poogie have composed their differences. Tell the pup from me that he should adopt the American attitude of being too proud to fight.

October 22nd, 1915: Rowan to Molly

Many thanks for your letter. I am so glad to hear that you are established at Newnham and beginning to feel at home. You will find it rather slow at the beginning among a crowd of strange girls, but one very soon makes friends at a College. You are a very lucky girl with your two rooms; I have a third of a bedroom at the end of a small cottage, and our mess is in a kitchen of another cottage, "mais c'est la guerre." The other end of our sleeping cottage is full of old ladies, and other old lady refugees – they must sleep about four deep, I should think – and they have about ten thousand old cronies in the village; the only way to their portion of the building is through our room, which owns three doors, so at all hours, whether in bed or out of bed, or partly one and partly the other, some door is thrust open, and some old lady hobbles in with a general "bon jour," to three partly clothed and astonished bachelors. This was wont to embarrass us a little at the start, but we now take our corridor existence quite philosophically.

Your mother sent me an excellent cake the other day, which arrived at tea time, when we were entertaining the Commanding Officer in our little mess, and was received with great acclamation, we "fired knives and presented arms," or rather hands, and dispersed it rapidly.

Glad to hear Thornley has got R.F.A., I think it is really the most interesting branch.

Billy and I have been endeavouring to convey to each other our whereabouts, but the wily censor must have snaffled one of my letters to him. We have, however narrowed it down to about ten miles. I rather like "fighting" in France when one is outside the firing line, but will probably be easily satisfied, not to say surfeited when I get to the trenches.

October 25th, 1915: Billy to Jack

Many thanks for your long and interesting letter, I was very glad to hear from you at last, but I can easily understand from your account of your manifold occupations that you have little time for letter-writing. You sound as if you were attempting more than it is within the capacity of any normal school-boy to do. I thought I was pretty hard worked when I was training this battery, and I had to do pay-sergeant, quartermaster sergeant, farrier, and countless other things connected with a battery which you wouldn't understand, as well as my own proper work of training them for war, but it was child's play to what you have taken on. I found that by dint of getting up at 6 a.m. and working till 12 midnight with short intervals for meals in those strenuous days I could just about keep abreast of the work, if I put in six hours on Sunday; but I gather that you don't have any meals, and go to bed about once a month. The life out here is really a very pleasant rest. I have now trained my officers and NCOs sufficiently to take a good deal of the routine work off my shoulders, and I can devote most of my time to my proper job, namely fighting the battery and devising schemes to down the wily Hun.

You will have had doubtless all my news from your mother, which doesn't amount to as much nowadays as would keep her stenographer[19], I believe that is the correct technical term, working overtime. Cheeroh

October 26th, 1915: Thornley to Molly
Buckerell Lodge, Exeter

My dear Molly,

I am most awfully sorry for neglecting you like this but the fact of sending off a parcel has almost proved too much for me, I have been trying to do it for a long time but hitherto failed. I enclose the original letter I wrote to you. Please don't be disappointed at the "parvum in multo" which I am sending you because it really is much easier to despatch a big thing than a small one.

How are you getting along? I am going fine. There has been an awfully good fellow sent down to us from the Cheshires, he knew Rowan there.

My horse had no name when I arrived so seeing that she was of the feminine persuasion and had a very strong will of her own I decided to take the liberty of calling her after you, "Molly." Her number is 84. She refuses any jump that she can possibly avoid, and is generally a great comfort to my soul.

The only point where the likeness breaks down is that you were always anxious to keep me in my place, while she seems to be only desirous of getting me out of it. She is however a staid old woman of 11 years.

Best love and wishes, Your loving bro, Thornley

---

[19] Lady Woods engaged a secretary who typed out each letter as it was received, so that copies could be distributed to other family members.

October 29th, 1915: Rowan to Meg

Thanks for parcel… The reason for these gigantic fortifications is the life we live out here. We are never out of mud varying from three inches to two feet.

The only places where we avoid mud is in the shell holes, where we get into water. My feet and legs were wet yesterday from 10 a.m. until I got back with a night digging party at 2.45 a.m. this morning. Our chief job while we are in reserve is to supply parties for working at the parapets of the trenches. This work has to be done at night, as it is open to the enemy's view by day. We start at 7.30 p.m., and it takes us half an hour to work our way to the old trenches for half a mile, which are liquid mud to the knees. Then we get into a main communication trench which is fairly good where there are no new shell holes. We feel our way along this in the dark, bumping from muddy side to muddy side. The pace must of course be very slow, or the company would lose touch in the rear and take all kinds of wrong turnings. We then thread our way to the spot assigned for our work, which has been inspected by some one or more of us officers the same afternoon. Then the men get their shovels and half go over the parapet in front, and half over the parados behind. Last night as soon as we got over the front about three night lights were sent up and fell among us; we got down into the narrow trench immediately and lay there for about ten minutes, while a burst of bullets came rattling about. When things quieted down we got out and started our work of piling earth up against the parapet, but every now and then another burst of fire would necessitate another dive in. Of course their shooting in the dark was only chance work, but they nearly scored some lucky flukes.

We go into the firing line on Monday, but I believe at a fairly quiet place.

1st November, 1915: Thornley to Molly

My dear Molly,

Thank you very much for your letter. I really must caution you against these frivolous and dissipated evenings which you seem to have been spending. My dear you will wear yourself out and I really must protest.

I took my first Church Parade yesterday and acquitted myself with great distinction at same. It was a Wesleyan Methodist performance and was highly interesting to me, because I had never been to one before. The Minister was the most arrant blighter that I ever came across in my life, I was thinking that his neck could be likened to a bull, both in shape and from the fact that it needed wringing.

I also had a letter from Billy but as it concerned nobody but myself and the steps I was to take about my transfer I decided not to send it home to be typed, for all the world to see.

I am getting to know a fairish deal about gunnery and battery tactics in the field and I think that once through my course I ought not to need much more except experience but I am kindly and firmly informed that everyone feels that at first but that they soon find out how little they know when they start for real.

November 2nd, 1915: Billy to Molly

Many thanks for your letter. The fire brigade sounds very exciting, but I should go sick, if I were you, any night there is a real fire, or failing that, turn the hose on to yourself, you can easily excuse this on the grounds of inaccurate aim, and it at least insures that you don't get burnt yourself, which is the main thing. When you rise to a position of command, as you are sure to do, you might encourage your squad by exhorting them to pull up their hose!

Your mother sent me his typed copy of Rowan's letter to you, and I thought his description of a French billet very true to life. Me having a bath was at one time one of the most popular shows in a certain village in Northern France. The spectators, which consisted of the entire population of the village, even going the length of pointing out to me various portions of my anatomy which I had omitted to wash, which, though kindly meant, was irritating. That, however, was a long time ago. I have long since forsaken baths and such like luxuries of an effete civilisation. Fort mit dem bad. A long abstinence from water has a curious effect which I have never noticed before, or else I was so small when I did notice it that I forgotten it. For the first fortnight you get steadily dirtier and dirtier till you reach a point at which you stick for a week or ten days, and then, to my astonishment and delight, you begin to get cleaner. It's a curious phenomenon, and I have discovered no satisfactory explanation. I am thinking of writing to Sir Almroth Wright about it.

I was sorry to hear that you were knocked out in the second round of the Tournament[20], but it was jolly good getting into it, unless you by any chance drew a bye in the first round, but I will not press for an answer to that question, as they say in Parliament. By playing on hard courts all winter you will indeed be a terror next summer, but I don't mind taking you on for a bob for all that. After all if I'm alive next summer I ought to have lots of bobs to chuck about. I think we will finally wind up the watch on the Rhine about next July, but don't go telling people I said so, as it might prejudice recruiting. All we want now, is fine weather and a fair chance. Cheeroh.

November 2nd, 1915: Rowan to Meg

Very many thanks for all the things you have sent me… I arrived in the reserve trenches last Sunday, as I wrote you, and found a pretty cosy dugout, new and comfortable. I got rations up to my firing line party myself the same night as I wished to make sure that they would arrive in the right place. We started at 7o'c, and arrived at 10.30. I pitied the men carrying heavy and awkward boxes and other parcels on a pitch dark night, and sliding in the mud, and going head and stern first into ditches at every step or so. They are wonderful fellows and stuck it

---

[20] Tennis

out so well that I got them each a tot of rum, which is a great event in Tommy's life out here.

The next day I walked up to the firing line to see what I could do for them, and to my great disgust it was there and then arranged by a majority of three officers to one that the reserve billet should be taken in turns; in consequence I was detained up there, and a brother officer sent down for a rest. Now I have only got the job every third day. I would like to bring home to you what the fire trenches are like, but I don't think I really could. You are never anywhere less than calf deep in liquid, or rather semi-solid mud, except when you are up to your thighs in water.

There is no way of draining them in this flat country, and we have no pumps. The trenches are not much more than wide enough to let you push through, cannoning against the sides from one shoulder or elbow to another. There is barely enough water to drink, all hand carried, and no clean water for washing available.

When it rains, as it started to do the night I went in, you sit wet through, or else you wet your waterproof or coat, which is practically all you can carry up to sleep in, except in one blanket. Everything gets wet eventually and you live and sleep in wet clothes, which of course you never can change, as you cannot carry a change in your pack. Gradually the mud, from much trampling, gets semi-solid and sticky, and it takes a really powerful exertion to drag your foot and leg out and place it in front as you go along. It takes me two hours to walk down our half company front (200 yards), and visit the sentries in their bays; and after I have done it, I am as tired as if I had performed a route-march of six hours in full marching order. One cannot get along without pushing and supporting oneself against the sides, so one's hands are always invisible from mud. I can see none of the cloth of my clothing. Finally, one eats mud with all one's food, as it is impossible to prevent its penetrating in. The curious thing about it is that I am very fit and well, although I would not have valued my life at a day's purchase if things had been brought to my mind before experiencing them.

The enemy opposite us are very quiet; in fact for the last few days I suspect that neither shivering side has had the heart to fire a shot other than a mere formality. The only real danger we are in, is that the dugout will collapse and smother one, as has happened in various cases, or that the trench walls will bury one as one feels one's way along them. My life was saved by getting hold of a pair of waders made of rubber or some composition of the same, which reach up to the thigh, and are dished out to the men as trench stores. They have kept my feet and legs dry the whole time. It is all the result of living in this flat country, where a shower of rain turns dry summer ditches into three foot winter canals. I am writing this from reserve where I am back again for another evening, and comparatively comfortable, having had my first wash for two days.

Your last cake and chocolate, which I saved for the trenches, were greatly appreciated, and the cake is – or was – the best we have chewed up yet. Many thanks; the tin boxes are also very useful for keeping things in trenches.

We have had a few casualties from bullets, and a few from land slides when the trenches or dugouts collapsed, but nothing serious. The second officers' dugout, which I inhabited with Halsey, collapsed, fortunately when we were not in it, and we had to take in turns to sleep with the sergt. major last night when off duty. I am looking forward to a nice sleep to-night in my own "little grey home," but something will probably occur to prevent it. Well, I am wonderfully fit for a tropical veteran, and a cold in my head, which afflicted me in dry billets, has disappeared since my clothes grew chronically wet, and I sleep in an ooze of mud. I believe we go back again next week to billets for another week, and after that I think the normal winter forty-eight hour spell in the trenches will be resumed, as no men could stick present conditions for longer. The Artillery are lucky in being speciously accommodated behind the trenches.

November 2nd, 1915: Billy to Meg

Very many thanks for all the things you have sent me, which came to hand all right: one parcel of cake, chocolate, and matches; one parcel of puttees, socks, and handkerchiefs (3); and one parcel of ski boots. The boots and puttees came just at the right time, as I'm afraid the weather has broken badly now, it has been raining for the last two days, and doesn't look like stopping for some time yet. The handkerchiefs also will be most useful.

I have had a letter from Blaker, Thornley's major, in which you'll no doubt be pleased to hear that he designated Thornley as a good lad, but as I feared, he shows no inclination to transfer him to Christchurch. However, I haven't yet heard from Curling, who may put things all right. Blaker, however, says that he anticipated no difficulty in getting Thornley posted to this Division.

The fact is that Blaker, who is a splendid fellow, had the misfortune to be born a German subject. His real name is Reichwald, and there was the devil and all of a fuss about him in the papers some time ago. He was out here, on the Staff, I think, but had to be sent home, as Joffre himself protested himself against having a German born subject on the British Staff. It's awfully bad luck on Blaker, who is as patriotic really as I am myself, but you will see the delicacy of my position in writing to him to have Thornley removed from his care. He probably sees anti-German significance in any suggestion of this sort, and naturally resents it, but of course, as you know, that side of the question would influence no one with any common sense.

Please don't say a word of this to Thornley, though he probably knows all about it. As a fact, Blaker is one of the cleverest officers we have.

I was very much amused at your encounter with the Editor of the *Irish Times*, he should have replied that as long as you did the shooting he wouldn't have considered himself in danger, but I suppose that would have been discourteous. I was awfully sorry when I saw that Carson[21] had resigned, I believe he's the only strong man left in political circles -- like Robert's description of Venizelos[22], the only man with both brains and guts.

What you say about the tactical situation is perfectly correct, and well illustrated by your diagram, but in any prognostication about the war there is one important element that you omit, and that is the weather. In a low-lying country like this, once the rainy season has set in, it is physically impossible to prosecute important operations of war on a large scale, the infantry can't advance against even a weak line however thoroughly the way has been prepared by Artillery, if at every step they sink into mud above their knees, and this is no exaggeration. Going down to the trenches the other day, I had to pull out each foot with both hands to get along at all, so you can imagine my rate of progression. We are on one wing of the salient in your sketch, and are doing no more at present than holding as many of the enemy as possible on our front, and prevent them being withdrawn to reinforce other points.

To do this of course we have to go for them every now and again, but I still think that all hope of a general advance is over until the spring. However, I hope you're right.

I haven't heard from Rowan for some time, and think the Censor must have collared one of his letters to me. We have been trying to arrange a meeting, and he probably gave his position away too definitely. I got your enclosure of his letter to Molly, his description of a billet is very true to life. A pal of mine on the Staff came to me the other day in woeful depression; it seems that his Chief, who had retired before the war and taken up politics, now considers it necessary to keep his hand in on somebody. So every night after dinner his wretched Staff have to sit round and listen to long political dissertations from the aforesaid Chief, who regards them in the light of his constituents. I roared with laughter when he told me this, wasn't a bit sympathetic, saying it was a small price to pay for his position on the gilded Staff. This didn't seem to console him a bit, in fact he seemed a bit envious of my comparative peace, and went away looking a bit thoughtful. It is incidents like this that help to lighten a soldier's life.

I am enclosing you a document that I received from my Colonel. I am I admit, a little diffident about asking you to do anything in this matter, as I know how busy you are with similar organizations among other things, but the point is that I do not want my Battery to suffer through my having omitted to provide myself with a wife. I don't think it ought to entail very much work, and it would be distinctly politic if Thornley is going to join this Division. If you feel inclined to do anything about it you might write to Mrs. Fasson (our General's wife) at the

---

[21] Sir Edward Carson resigned as Attorney General 19 October 1915 to become leader of the Opposition.
[22] Eleftherios Venizelos, Prime Minister of Greece brought Greece into the war on the side of the Allies.

address given, and get into touch with her. If you tell her you are my sister, it will explain everything, but please don't hesitate to say no if you'd rather not. None of my officers have wives, otherwise I wouldn't have bothered you at all, and I don't know any person of the female persuasion sufficiently well to ask her to undertake the honorary duties. It might lead to complications in the future. I expect they only want to coordinate all their efforts, and you needn't do very much really, but it would be better for my battery if they were represented on the Committee.

November 5th, 1915: Rowan to Robert

Just a line this morning following my letter to Margaret to let you know that I am feeling very chirpy this morning. The sun has come out, and I have had a whole night's sleep and a shave and have aired my only shirt, so that I feel like a young Guardsman in Piccadilly. I go back to the line this afternoon.

You may imagine what the country is like here when men have been stuck all night buried to the waist in mud in our principal communication trench. One of our officers, a man from Bray, a barrister in Dublin has just got the military cross for gallantry on 25th September, we are all awfully pleased. He saved a whole company of the Welsh on our right by voluntarily bringing them out the word to retire.

The whole battalion has been served out with thigh boots (rubber) to-day, which will save our lives and help the particular fortunes of rubber estates; I hear good news of mine[23]. If Margaret has not already sent out the trench stockings tell her not to mind about them, as I hear they are not much good. The waders they have dished us out here are fine things, specially strapped at ankle and knee to prevent us walking out of them. Tell Margaret a suit of warm underclothing might be sent to me now – one only, as we can exchange it at baths at the base. Remember about the compass, it is essential to have a luminous one with a directing arrow, when patrolling in front of the trench.

November 9th, 1915: Rowan to Meg

Thanks for the trench stockings and India rubber socks. The latter are splendid; the former I am sending back, as they are too short to be of any use. The only waders that are any good must come up well to the top of the thighs, as we often have to wade thigh deep.

We are now back after eight days in the firing line, and have a nice little billet. All four of us sleep and eat in one room, but it has a fine open grate, and we have lots of fuel and logs to keep a cheery fire going. We are just on the line of the Artillery, and get a dose of shrapnel now and then when they are looking for

---

[23] Mardenshaw Rubber Estates – mentioned below and also in *An Irishman in Malaya* (see bibliography)

them. We spend most days and nights taking parties in front to repair the line and clear the trenches; the latter is rather a difficult matter, as the ground surface is below water level. They got on to my party with shrapnel to-day, but we successfully retired to cover without any casualties, and resumed work when the agony had passed. Later in the day I was up in an observation post in a tree with a gunner officer, and saw them strafe the German line in great style. The Huns, however, got a few shells very close to his battery. We shall in all probability be back in the firing line on Monday, but I hope in somewhat better trenches.

Tell Robert the compass is top-hole, and should guide me splendidly on patrol. The patrols rather tickle up one's nerves. We have to creep out at a saphead, and crawl over to the German lines and listen, and try to see.

Every now and then the Very lights go up and one has to sit still like a pointer. Every instant one is apprehensive of meeting an enemy patrol, when a fight in the dark with bombs and revolvers would take place. I have not met one yet, thank goodness. A parcel from Findlater's with fruit, cream and tongue came, for which many thanks, also an anonymous parcel of books from Greene's Library, which I expect came from Helen Fottrell, and which are most welcome both to me and the company. I have not yet got into touch with Billy, and do not expect that either of us would be able to get away for some time.

10th November 1915: Thornley to Molly

My dear Molly,

Thank you so much for all the letters I have not yet acknowledged. Don't be put out about me in the cold, I am used to it by now. The first nip came rather suddenly and consequently I felt it, also I have the earliest riding school and have to get up at 6.30 in the morning which makes things feel a good bit warmer. I have a very nice warm jacket of which I am deeply appreciative.

If I were you I should take my fireman's (or woman's) axe with which no doubt you are supplied and break that old hydrant and all the emergency hydrants of which I am sure there are three into such smithereens that fire practice could no longer be continued, you could then as Betty says watch the plumber mending them and exhort him to "pull up his hose."

You will no doubt be pleased to hear that I have again got hold of my dear old Molly, and that I ride in comfort and elevation (she stands 16 hands two inches) not to mention pleasure.

I really cannot write any more. It is now 10.15 p.m. and I am rather tired as I have been at it since 8.00 this morning. Your ever loving brother, Thornley

November 11th, 1915: Rowan to Meg

Just a line to let you know that I am fit and well. We go back to the firing line to-morrow, but only for four days. It is rather nice in a way, as they work us very hard here. We have been taking parties up day and night with material etc., dug-outs, and building same. We are building very good ones now of stout wood and corrugated iron well set in sand-bags, but have to raise everything about them three feet above ground level to keep them dry.

There is really quite as much danger outside, as they spray all communication trenches and working parties with shrapnel and trench mortars, so we are not displeased to get back.

The only thing I really mind much is the patrol work, -- crawling on one's belly between the lines, and palpitating periodically at nothing.

I enclose a letter from Martin for safe keeping, it contains good news of Mardenshaw, which I reared and practically with my own hand laboured it to grow.

The rubber socks will be on their trial to-morrow, and I shall let you know.

November 13th, 1915: Billy to Meg

Many thanks for both your letters dated 8th, and 9th, also for the parcel of tinned fruit, tongue and cream, which arrived safely. I can't think what happened to my pyjamas, they must have been pinched en route. I never got the letter in which you acknowledged the receipt of Lt. Reinacker, or giving me Rowan's address, I wonder what can have happened to it, the Censor does open a very small proportion of the outward-bound letters, but it is extremely unlikely that he would stop it, he would only erase the part he objected to; it may turn up, but I can't think why it should have gone astray. Nobody would take the trouble to pinch a letter.

Thanks very much for taking up the duties connected with the R.A. 23 Div. comforts, I hope it won't involve much trouble or expense, though I will defray any of the latter you incur. I was very much amused by Mrs. Cleary's (I always forget the name of your cook) comments on Michael[24], his appearance, and his importance in relation to the War, I wonder if he is anywhere near me. He's in the R.F.C., isn't he?

Rowan's letters, which you enclose, are strong corroborative evidence of my contention that anything like a general advance is impossible till the Spring.

Your last letter shows me that I am roughly within eight miles of him, but I have not been able to get away to see him yet, the fact being that I daren't leave the battery for so long till things have settled down a bit.

After nearly a month of comparative peace we have had a very unpleasant experience during the last three days. There is a battery just alongside and a little in front of me here, and by some mischance the Huns spotted it last Wednesday, I think by means of an aeroplane so they opened on it with a field battery, but didn't do much damage. They were shooting a bit wild and we got some of their shells, three bursting just outside our tool-shed mess, and wounding in the thigh one of our servants who was sawing wood. Next day, Thursday, they turned on a 15cm. howitzer battery, and gave us the devil of a doing, firing about 100 shells

---

[24] Michael Lloyd, the butler's son.

into and around this battery position between 10 a.m. and 12.30. One poor devil had his head blown clean off, and three others were wounded, including my battery cook. During a pause about 12 o'clock when I thought they had finished, I walked over to this other battery to see what damage had been done, and with the other B.C. was examining one of his guns which had been slightly damaged, when off they started again, and the very first shell burst just in front of this gun. The concussion was terrific and blew me straight on to the back of a gunner who was sitting inside the gun-pit, but by an extraordinary chance nobody was touched, and beyond a headache next day I am feeling none the worse. In the afternoon I blew a village of theirs to smithereens where I suspected there was a battery, by way of retaliation, and they haven't worried us since.

Owing to the unfortunate wounding of the cook the men couldn't have a hot meal as usual, and when I asked one of my Bombardiers how he liked the shelling that morning, his only comment was - "It's a bit thick, sir, when they knock out the cook."

I'm glad to hear the pup is acting as a health tonic for you. I am filled with admiration of his tactical skill in defying Poogie and the next-door dog from the back-drawing room window. "He'd have made a great soldier, the creature" - to quote Mrs. Cleary. I must refer you to your second son Jack for your temerity in correcting me for saying that Molly had joined the local fire brigade. Considering that she is at Newnham, she couldn't have joined a more local one than the Newnham one. I have already written to Jack at some length on this subject, and I am sure he will agree with me.

November 14th, 1915: Rowan to Meg

This from the firing line again. I started off last Friday, equipped as I thought, to meet four days in trenches without a damp foot. Your rubber socks sandwiched between woollen ones, and over all trench waders. Fate ruled otherwise, however, as half way up to trench at the head of my platoon, I put my left leg in a hole thigh deep, and filled my left leg with water. That night after emptying my boot and removing the water and damp socks, one leg was nice and warm, at the start at least, and one freezing cold. The next morning coming off duty at 6 a.m. I thought I would wait till light before taking off my boots, and sat down to read by candle light. The candle was on my bed, and I woke up later putting a fire out with an empty bottle, and not comprehending what I was doing for some time. I then got it out, narrowly escaped suffocating, and lost half of my waterproof sheet and blanket.

We have the Huns well in hand here. I inspected all the wire in front of our parapet last night, and not a shot was fired. When they hurled over trench mortars we strafe them with our Artillery, and they soon chuck it.

I want socks badly; this life in rubber boots wears the heels out in no time, and we can't get them dried. Please send three pairs knee high as possible, they cannot be too long. The weather now is frosty and bright, a great contrast to our first couple of nights in, when it was raining.

November 17th, 1915: Thornley to Molly

Dear Molly,

I am most awfully sorry for not writing before but my course has begun and we are working pretty hard for a change. The "personnel" of the whole mess has changed practically entirely since I came and I think a good deal for the better but one cannot tell as one knows so little of the people here.

Thank you very much indeed for your kind present of a pair of mittens. I wore them the Saturday after they arrived on subalterns 9 a.m. drill and was the only one I have heard of who kept his fists warm, this, considering that the sleet was coming down in volleys, was hardly surprising.

The weather here is something cruel, the cold is enough to make a man curse his God. I will give you an instance. I have six thicknesses of blanket above and five below me when I sleep and a muffler round my neck and I count myself jolly lucky if I am only moderately cold when I get up. That coupled with the fact that I have to get up in the dark, dress and go on an empty stom. to riding school is enough to finish me off. Of course once at work in the school it is all right and quite warm.

I expect to be dismissed shortly in fact next Friday should see me through. I have a beautiful horse whose only fault is a rather uncomfortable trot when stirrups are not used, I think on the whole though that I would rather have had "Molly."

Ever your loving brother, Thornley

November 25th, 1915: Rowan to Meg

I have received the parcels all right, and the contents are very welcome, the matches were first rate, but the cakes carbonised or carbonated, or whatever it is they do, much quicker. I also received a very noble parcel from Gracie[25] which contained soda bread and butter, and all manner of luxuries. The mess passed her a vote of thanks nem. con.

The expression of sympathy in your letter reminds me of the expression of one of my men in a letter which I censored addressed to a mother who had apparently been commiserating with him. He thanked her for her "softness." We had a pretty hard time for a month, but we are now in the lap of luxury. We are Division in reserve for a month, about three to five miles back, and each officer has got a comfortable bed. I never felt fitter, and indeed in the trenches when wet and shivering I felt as fit as ever I did, although astonished each day that some terrible illness did not develop. I was afraid to say how well I felt until I had got safely out.

---

[25] Cousin Grace Morrow, née Shaw, who lived in Strandtown, Belfast. Her Shaw relations served in the Royal Navy.

We are hard at work every day here, drilling the men and practising the arts and wiles of war. It is the real stuff, and much more interesting than the dull life in the reserve in England.

The snow boots arrived all right, and I hope you got the trench stocking I sent home.

We get ten days leave after three months in France, but as we go into the trenches again on December 24th, I shall probably not get home till the end of January.

I got the stove, razor etc., from Robert yesterday, which were all a great success, except that methylated spirit for warming the stove has not so far been attainable; our cook, however, encircled the burner with a rag steeped in paraffin, and all went well.

Our Division has got a great name, and having regard to the other Divisions with which we have recently been associated we expect some stirring times in the good old summer time.

I have not heard from Billy recently; if I knew where he was now, I might get a chance to go and see him.

Molly seems to be enjoying herself at Newnham.

November 29th, 1915: Billy to Molly

Many thanks for all your letters, I am afraid I have not written to you for some time. I'm glad you were not converted by the Suffragette, though I'm in favour of votes for qualified women, I do not consider blowing up public buildings as a convincing argument in favour of any political propaganda. I read and enjoyed enormously the "Ymn of 'Ate" and I believe it was written about one of the regiments I was very friendly with when they were on our part of the line. Anyhow it's an excellent description of how the Cockney treats the Hun. Good-humoured, tolerant contempt is his attitude.

I think you ought to tell the Captain of your Fire Brigade - it will carry more weight if you say it comes from Captain Shaw - that the policy of crying "Wolf" is a fatal one to the efficiency of the force under her command. You seem to spend your time trekking about the corridors with a hose. When the real fire comes, absit omen[26], you will all be in hot baths, and consequently you will all get into hot water, (loud and prolonged laughter, in which the Major joined heartily). You must pardon my high spirits, bit I have been given a week's leave which is to start on Jan 2nd, so if all goes well I will be home on Jan 3rd.

I'm not a rich man, but I would have given as much as 5/- to have heard the debate conducted by the third year Moral Science Girls on "The man who strives to develop to the full his own personality, best serves his fellow men." It must have been as good as a Pantomime. Do they allow you to laugh?

---

[26] "evil spirits keep off" or might be translated as "touch wood"

G.O.M. stands for Grand Old Man, quite right. The G.O.M. in question was a young feller of the name of Gladstone. When you can spare a moment from winding up or unrolling that blooming fire-hose, you might profitably glance through a contemporary history, in which I think you would probably find him mentioned.

I was glad to hear of the regeneration of Patricia. I expect to find her glowing with a "mens sibi conscia recti"[27] when I get home.

November 29th, 1915: Thornley to Molly

My dear Molly,

Thank you very much for your letter and the present, which you say you are sending. I forget whether I told you that your namesake played the dirty on me on Saturday.

With infinite pains and trouble I managed to make her jump a post and rail fence about 3 feet high. She cleared it by about 3 ft. she was so anxious not to hack her shins on it, and then was so pleased with herself that she went away at a hard gallop along the bottom of a valley. This would have been very well if it had not been for the fact that she insisted on going up the slope diagonally on the left. Knowing her for a good hunting mare and feeling that she knew her own business best, I let her go. The unfortunate part being that she crossed a spring in the side of the hill, her foot slipped and she and I went point over tip together. Luckily I went further than she did and although she rolled a good deal she did not catch me but I landed on my shoulder and the side of my head. I got up at once and started leading her down to the bottom of the incline. It was only when I had gone about 60 yards down, that I felt queer and sick, and knocked up.

Well, well, I am none the worse and that is one in the tale of those jumps that got to make a horseman, and after all it wasn't the old marc's fault. Thank goodness she was a good deal less perturbed than I was myself or I don't know what the Major would have said, it is really his horse and he is very particular about her.

If you are going home as soon as you say I shall almost certainly see you when I get leave as I shall probably do about Xmas, I am waiting to Rhys to know when they break up at Shrewsbury - I have given up trying to get information from my respective and respected brothers.

We are not in tents or huts, but in a private house where the 18th Battery officers are quartered, it is attached to the barracks and really belongs to them.

The reason why it is so cold is that the old man (Col. Reid was his name), who built it, was afraid of the police, and consequently had to have on an average 8 doors to each room, on the ground floor there are 42 doors (this is solid fact) and very few fire-places. I think the old buffer was mad, but his old butler who managed our mess as head waiter says that he was a very fine gentleman and a

---

[27] "a mind conscious of rectitude"

very good officer, and as a proof of the first affirms that he never allowed anything less aristocratic than claret to be drunk at dinner, and of the second that he is now in a responsible post in the War Office!

This puts me in mind of the story of the Turkish sniper who was captured. His story was that he was paid a bounty for every officer he shot, increasing in proportion to the rank of his victim, but that if he bagged an officer with red tabs on his collar or a red hat (denoting staff appointment) he was paid the sum of £2 (or equivalent in Turkish money) and put in prison for an indefinite period !!

Your ever-loving brother, Thornley S. Woods

November 30th, 1915: Billy to Thornley

I was very glad to get your letter and to hear that you are getting on so well, I was also glad to hear that the officers have changed since you arrived first. I met a young fellow called Thorpe out here at dinner the other night who told me he had been at Exeter with you; it seems he came from the shop, and was only waiting until he was of military age to come out. Things are going very well out here. We have had a lot of Artillery activity in the last fortnight, and I think we are gradually getting on top of them. They started the same by systematically shelling all down our line and gave us a very unpleasant time, so lately we have been having organized retaliation on all their gun positions. Yesterday we had a combined "strafe" and I think I managed to get a distinct hit on one of their batteries that has been very troublesome lately, as there was a distinct and separate second explosion after one of our shells burst. Anyhow he shut up then and hasn't fired since, but to-day another blighter shelled our mess, but only with little pip-squeaks, i.e. 7.7 cm., and did practically no damage. It was really only a nasty display of temper, I don't think they have spotted the battery position yet. I have been given a week's leave which will start on Jan 2nd, so I hope to be home about the 3rd; if you could manage to get a bit of leave then it would be rather nice, as I should like to have a talk with you, but I suppose you will get your leave at Christmas time.

I am going to try and get down to see Rowan sometime soon. He has gone into Divisional Reserve for a month, so his discomfort in the trenches is over for the present. I am very glad for his sake, as the trenches are appalling in this weather. It is bitterly cold out here, but I hope we have a hard winter, as it is much more comfortable than rain when you live in a dug-out. I have come slowly to the conclusion that, however unpropitious the signs, the Germans are beat. I don't mean to say by this that we have not got a long and tough job in front of us, but it rapidly resolving itself into a question of time and money. They have reached the high water mark in numbers, practically every German we kill now is irreplaceable. Their morale is deteriorating, and there is no doubt from prisoners; statements, captured documents etc., that the civilian population is beginning to feel the pinch. They have been kept up heretofore by the stories of great victories about to be achieved by Germany, and the longer the victories are deferred the greater will be the collapse; so stick to your gun-drill and your laying, and we will 'ere long drink "Hoch der Kaiser" in the best beer restaurant in the Unter den Linden can provide. You, of course, will pay for the beer.

November 30th, 1915: Billy to Meg

I got your letter from the North all right. I'm glad you gave Cousin Lizzie one of my photographs, I particularly wanted her to have one. This is to say that you can knock off socks and chocolate for the present, as I have now an ample stock of both commodities. It is splendid the work you're doing for the R.A., it's really awfully good of you to undertake it at all, but there's no doubt that a little private enterprise adds enormously to the comfort of the men.

Thornhill, who lives in Galway, is trying to get ten days leave on the grounds of the distance he has to go, so if he succeeds I will make a similar effort on the grounds that "it is a long, long way to Tipperary" - if I put it in quotation marks it will commit me to nothing, as there's no denying its truth, and I need not specify that I, personally, am going to stop in Dublin. Also a little human touch like this often has a wonderfully mollifying effect on the adamant hearts of G.H.Q.

I'm sorry I told you about that shell if it upset you, these little incidents are bound to happen occasionally, so you need not worry.

Robert with the pup must be a great sight. I have written to Thornley to try and get leave at the same time as I do, but don't know if he will manage it. I expect you would like him home at Christmas.

November 30th, 1915: Billy to Jack

Thank you so much for the long and interesting letters that I have received from you with such regularity of late; I suppose your multitudinous duties leave you little time for letter writing. I wrote to you some time ago on the subject of your meticulous exactitude in expression.[28] I wonder if you ever received it.

Things are going wonderfully well out here, with just sufficient excitement to keep you from getting bored. I hope you and Bobby are both going strong and enjoying yourselves. I am getting a short leave home on or about Jan 2nd, so I hope to see you all then. I presume the whole family will be at home then with the possible exception of Thornley. I am going to try and go down to see Rowan sometime soon, he has gone into Divisional Reserve, but I must not mention the name of the place. I have written to him to try and get leave then too. It would be indeed splendid if we could all be at home together. I have had numerous letters from Molly, she is splendid at writing, and seems to spend most of her time extinguishing imaginary fires.

Love to Bobby.

---

[28] Billy is encouraging Jack to become a lawyer.

December 5th, 1915: Rowan to Meg

We are back in it again, or at any rate on the brink, being Brigade in Reserve of our Division in the trenches.

Last Thursday evening, when well in and well under my blankets in a beautiful bed, sleeping torturously after an excellent dinner and a short attendance at a very lubricant sergeants' smoker, a long sinuous arm, snake-like and sinister, waving at the business end of it an urgent message received by telephone, obtruded itself on my rosy slumbers. After opening my eyes and eying the fearsome flapper suspiciously, and trying to believe it was a dream, or, at worst, a phantom, the results of a fortnight's ardent indulgence in the arts of peace, I clutched it nervously and found it all too real: -- "The battalion will move to the trenches at 7 a.m., officers' valises to be at H.Q. at 5.30 a.m." etc., you can imagine how pleased I was. The next day we marched 18 miles in the rain in full marching order, and yesterday arrived here, back to the merry shell zone again.

After being allotted a very poor barn to sleep and live in, we of B. Coy prowled round and found an intact corner of an old Brewery, where we have made ourselves comfortable. There is still three weeks rest due to us, and if we get it in January I shall be due then for eight days leave, and may get it at the same time as Billy gets his, which would be top hole.

I have got a bit of a cold, but am expecting it to yield to a dose of the trenches.

You might send along another cake and some chocolate for the trenches. I don't think Findlater's parcels are worthwhile, as we can get things like that at odd places here without postage.

December 7th, 1915: Billy to Meg

I have received your letter of the 3rd. The list of the things coming for Christmas sounds most appetising. I was just going to ask you to send us a boned fowl of some sort, such as you used to send me at school, but now I can think of nothing to add to what you are already sending.

Lady Sclater (pronounced Slatah) is no less a person than the wife of Lt. Gen. Sir Henry Sclater, Adjutant-General to the Forces, and second Military Member of the Army Council, also one of our most distinguished Gunners. He was my General in India when I was at Hyderabad, and a very nice fellow to boot. It's a pity she forestalled you in the *Irish Times*, but she is collecting for the whole of the Royal Artillery. It would be very nice of you if you have time to go and look up Mrs. Badham-Thornhill. He himself is going on leave sometime this month, probably to see the infant. If you meet him I can promise you quite an amusing half hour.

You will be sorry to hear that I was flooded out of my dug-out last Saturday night, in spite of all our efforts the water rose a foot above the level of the floor and defeated us. I am now quite comfortably installed in a room in a farm close by, but unluckily it has got no fire-place. However, the weather has been much milder of late. We have been very busy lately, having regular bombardments of the German lines practically every day. I got a direct hit on one of their batteries the other day, and blew up a gun emplacement, so we have got a bit of our own back. We have had regular duels with them, which are very exciting, and so far we seem to be well on top of them. I have been so busy that I have not been able to get away to see Rowan. I was about to start last Saturday, but was stopped at the last moment by a "Strafe." I am looking forward enormously to seeing you all in January.

December 13th, 1915: Rowan to Meg

We have just got back from a rather interesting part of the trenches for a week's repose. We had eight days rather strenuous work. The lines zig-zagged so much that it was very hard to tell at any given point where one's front lay. To make it harder the line had crumbled away, and was only held in isolated posts about 40 yards apart. It was quite on the cards at any moment of a patrol to find oneself short-circuited in to the Bosche lines. On one occasion on a pitch dark night I lost my whereabouts altogether, and for over an hour crossed from one line to the other, about forty yards, listening for a voice to give a clue as to which was the Hun and which our own line.

My orderly and servant, an egregious person called Thomas, who gets blind whenever he finds himself within a mile of a pub., was alternatively cocksure that he heard German and English in each line, also that "parties" were closing round us. Ultimately, in desperation, I pulled out Robert's compass, fixed the general direction of our line, barged on with revolver ready in one hand, and a stout ash plant in the other, and just as I put my head over the ruins of a parapet was relieved to hear in English a very forcible expression of his opinion of the war, the trenches, the weather, the food, and everything generally; each sentence prefixed, punctuated, and neatly rounded off by a verbal adjective which is beloved by Tommies, and which even Bernard Shaw would not dare to put into a play. Better not ask Robert or anybody else what it is.

One night we held a portion of the line where our salient converges on a Hun salient to a distance of only 15 yards. There is practically no cover. It is a post held on each side by about 16 men armed with bombs. Either side could wipe out the other with bombs in about five minutes if either started; the consequence is that neither side do anything but sit and talk to each other all day. When we were up there we persuaded a German to desert. Our O.C. Coy. went across to encourage him back. We made him as tight as a lord on a platoon's ration of rum. And what with that and joy getting out of the war, he sung like a lark all day and recommended his pals to come over too. He subsequently gave us information which enabled us to knock out a German brigade who were coming to relieve the firing line.

The men were all delighted with the prisoner, and I overheard one saying:- "Well, for over a year I swore I would brain the first German I saw, and there he was with his arms round my neck kissing me, and I even lighted his cigarette for him."

The bread and butter were much appreciated.

December 16th, 1915: Billy to Meg

All your parcels have arrived safely. Many thanks for them all, we are looking forward to a first class Christmas dinner, but I am looking forward still more to my leave. It is less than three weeks now. I regret to have to inform you that the extra day given to the Irish and Scotch officers is off for the present, but I trust it will be on again before I go on leave. If not, I will only get a trifle under seven days from the time I arrive in London until I have to leave again, however I suppose we are jolly lucky to get any at all.

I have had a letter from Blaker saying that Thornley's training is now complete, and that he may be sent out at any moment, so I have written to-night to our General asking him to do what he can to get Thornley posted to this Division. The rest we must leave in the lap of the gods. I should not be surprised, however, if they did not send him out here at all for some time, but posted him to one of the new Divisions they are raising at home, and make him help to train it. Thornley would probably be very sick at this, but I really think it would be the best thing for him, he is very young yet, and there will not be much doing out here till the Spring.

December 19th, 1915: Rowan to Meg

We have just completed a very pleasant week in rest billets, and start back to the trenches to-day.

Billy rode over yesterday and had lunch and dinner with us. He looked very fit and was in good form.

We had a great dinner of which the staple feature was your turkey skillfully warmed up. It was most excellent, and met with great approbation by the mess and the guests thereof. I think a goose similarly treated, and arriving about Dec. 28th when we change from the trenches, would have a most soothing effect.

If leave is going in the beginning of January I think I can work mine on the same day as Billy gets his, which will be very nice. Things are livening up a bit, though, and anything may happen to stop leave altogether; however we hope for the best. We are going into a new section of the trenches, which will be interesting, and I hope drier than our last effort.

December 20th, 1915: Billy to Molly

Many thanks for your letter, I am making this letter do for everyone, as you are all at home now except Thornley. Tell Johnnie I received his letter, with many thanks for same. I have written to your mother acknowledging all her parcels which were duly received, and we are now looking forward to a Christmas dinner worthy of all your efforts. I was very much surprised to hear that Thornley is coming out so soon. I have done all in my power to get him sent to this Division, and there the matter rests for the present. Between ourselves I wouldn't be a bit surprised if they were all sent to one of the new Divisions they are raising at home out of Derby's recruits. There is, as far as I know, no lack of officers out here at present, so if they come out now they would be supernumerary.

On Saturday last I rode over to a certain village and saw Rowan. His battalion was in reserve there, but went back to the trenches yesterday. I had lunch, tea, and dinner with them, and then rode back at dead of night to my own battery, a very perilous undertaking. I was arrested at one place as a spy, and detained in a barn until a very young, sleepy, and frightened second lieutenant was hauled out of bed to come and settle what was to be done to me. I was rather angry at first, but when the situation dawned on me I felt rather amused and eager to see what was going to happen. Well, he arrived, looked at me, saluted gravely, and then stood blinking, and hadn't the foggiest notion what to do next. So as it was getting late, and I was a bit tired, I decided to help him out, so I said in my fiercest voice - "What, sir, is the meaning of this outrage?" The poor little devil apologised profusely, and murmured something to the  effect that the sentry had to obey orders, and that it was better that six innocent persons should be put to some inconvenience than that one spy should escape. With that I agreed, but thought it well to drive home the point that a little display of intelligence on the part of the sentry wouldn't come amiss, pointing out that spies don't ride about on grey horses accompanied by orderlies, clattering about the high hard road at dead of night. I further pointed out that so far as my being a spy was concerned, he was no forrader, as up till then I had produced no proof of my identity, suggesting that he should go and rouse his Colonel, as he was obviously too junior and inexperienced to deal with such a delicate problem. This suggestion put the kybosh on it, he was so horrified at the mere idea that I had to laugh, and we parted amicably after more apologies from him, which were graciously accepted by me. So I got home with no damage except for the fact that my unaccustomed ride of sixteen miles took a piece of skin off that portion of my anatomy which in the days long since gone by was the recipient of the back and the bristles. While I was down I saw Rowan's second in command, and put in a strong word for his having leave at the same time as myself. The regiment expects to be back in Corps Reserve by Jan 1st so there is every chance that he will get it. It will be splendid if we are both home together, but the question that occurs to my mind is where are you going to put us all? I want you to stake out a claim for us on Patsy's room, most of my clothes are there already, and I know if I share a room with Rowan our things will get inextricably mixed up. I suppose at a pinch you could put a bed in the play-room, this would do me equally well if I have it to myself. I also want you to get hold of my plain clothes, sufficient for me to wear while I'm on leave – boiled shirts etc., – my fresh clothes are at Rathleigh, but I don't quite know what.

I am looking forward more than I can say to the comforts of a happy house again, and to seeing you all.

January 5th, 1916: Molly to Thornley

My dear Thor,

I am very sorry not to have written sooner but we have been very busy lately. Billy arrived home on Tuesday morning in an exhausted condition but is all right again now. Rowan arrived this morning and is at present asking if the bath is very wet and wondering if he will catch cold if he takes one. They are both very cheery and full of buck. We got your inebriated letter but of course we don't believe you are going to the front.

The weather here is vile. Rain and storm, storm and rain. By the way they caught three submarines, one of which was nestling on the Kish bank. You crossed that night by the only boat that left Ireland for England. We have since heard that the two night mails one from each side were the only communication held between the two countries during four days. So you can boast your courage and devotion to duty.

Patricia is at last well of the cold and is completing her cure by sleeping in my room where she rises and sets in record time. Jack and Bobby are as usual flourishing. I must stop as everybody is wanting things done and I have hardly time to breathe. With much love and best wishes,

Your loving sister, Molly

January 19th, 1916: Thornley to Molly

I omitted to mention in my last letter that I made some mistakes with my clothes I sent home, e.g. I should very much like another set of pyjamas. I'm sure you will be able to find one of mine lying about that is more or less intact.

Yesterday was a quiet day here for me at least. We fired about 30 rounds all day to retaliate against the Hun. In the afternoon I walked up to the O.P. with my B.P. and we could hardly see anything of the surrounding country. For that it was no earthly use taking on anything as we could not see where the shells were going. It is great fun to see our aeroplanes in the air with the Hun letting fly at them and getting about halfway.

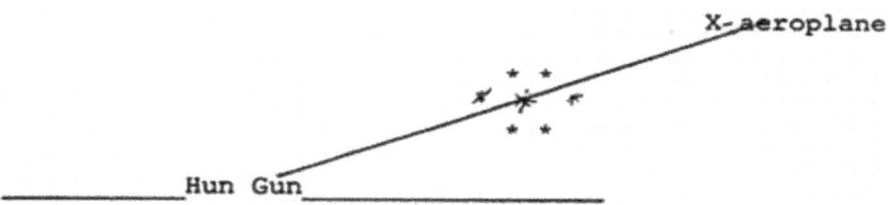

You see their line is quite correct, only from their old pop-gun, they cannot see how far the bursts are going.

Today I saw two of our lads up with the puffs going all round them, how the devil they escaped I don't know but I suppose it was not nearly so close as it looked. Anyway the "airbug" didn't seem to care a blow. He sailed backwards and forwards as if he was giving an exhibition flight at home.

The weather out here has been very mild, it rained yesterday, but it is lovely today. It is a beautiful day for the boys because even up here the bursts of the "Archies"[29] stay quite still for about 15 minutes before dispersing. So there can't be much air moving.

Give my love to all at home and get that tobacco contract on the move as quickly as possible because supplies are beginning to run low here.

Your ever loving brother Thornley.

January 23rd, 1916: Thornley to Molly

My dearest Molly

Thank you so much for your letter, it was sent on in a batch from Exeter. as all my things are because we have an excellent man there who takes no end of trouble with us.

I am very glad to hear you are over the R.N.'s room. Your hours last year were a scandal and you jolly well might learn that for little girls like you a golden rule is bed by 7.30 p.m. (known out here as "pip emma" which sounds so ludicrous that one might sympathise with the American who was going through a signalling course asking "who is Emma anyway and why pip her?").

Cheeroh and keep the home fires burning

Thornley

January 27th, 1916: Thornley to Molly

Thank you very much for your letter. I wrote home last night in the vain hope that my craze for letter writing would be satisfied. Ever since I came over here I seem to have been possessed by the awful intention of writing such quantities of letters that the replies would exceed all that could possibly be imagined if they came in a lump.

---

[29] An "Archibald" was a nickname for a certain kind of shell

For goodness sake drop the fire brigade! It cannot do you any good because with an efficient corps in the place it is almost a moral certainty that a fire will never take place, also with an efficient corps in the place you stand a better chance of remaining intact if you do not belong to that corps. It is better to be saved than to save. And you would never be forgiven if you did not risk your life in the flames if you were a member. Whereas if you did when you were not a member, the member who had to rescue you would probably be distinctly and justly annoyed. In the meanwhile you are risking death by cold in order to make yourself efficient to risk death on "der tag."

Again if a fire really does break out the fire brigade will arrive and politely but firmly place the amateurs in the background before getting to work. If these are not sufficient reasons to convince you I can say no more. I'm glad you are enjoying yourself and that the freshers are at last getting a look in on the entertaining line. If I were you I would undress one night, turn off your light and then rush about and shriek till the authority over whose devoted head you live could be heard on the stairs, you could then step into bed. When she came in you would be talking about fires (in your sleep, of course). She would counsel you to give it (the fire brigade) up and you could protest gently. This would be a tactful way of getting out of a difficult situation and could not possibly give offence to anyone.

Love and best wishes for a happy term. I suppose you are still studying the language of the Hun! Alas for feminine delicacy! Your loving brother

January 29th, 1916: Thornley to Molly

My dear Molly,
Thank you very much for your letter. I think you need have no fear of my taking unnecessary risks, it would do your heart good to see me gather up the skirts of my mac, and scuttle for shelter at the first suggestion of "Ppheeough ... pfitt" which is what a bullet says or "Wheeeeeee ..... " which is what a small shell says. Rude, aren't they!

Your remarks about "our common brothers" are true and to the point. I only hope that you don't couple to the adjective that other generally found with it in the Bible of "unclean," this might perhaps be unjust. Not that they are incapable of tricks of that description. Please don't bother about sending me out things, because although they are very nice, I am getting consignments from home and it is too much trouble for you.

The monotony of things out here was broken yesterday by the Bosch. He had a great strafe on out first and second line trenches and practically every battery for about ten minutes up and down the front was popping away for all it was jolly well fit. I had a talk with General Gough, the Irish cavalry man who commands the division of which we form a part of the artillery. He was a very decent man and full of fun. Of course I mention this en passant and négligé, etc., but I was really greatly honoured by the gentleman. Things are just the same today, there was a thick mist on and where I was up in the a.p. one could hardly see anything, consequently the Hun was still and I had a peaceful morning, he loosed a couple at an old battery towards midday but it was just their way of passing the time.

Loads of love. I hope you look well as a Babe in a Wood though I think Miss Gildard should go as the Babes and then you could be the Woods (ha!ha! Loud laughter during which part of the audience stood up).

Well, well a truce to these pleasantries. Keep the home fires going or burning, or whatever it is. Your loving brother, Thornley.

P.S. I have been drinking real rum, almost black, which turns red when you dilute it. I daresay the piratical feeling which it has induced has had some influence on this letter.

February 9th 1916: Thornley to Molly

My dear Molly,

What a dear you are to write to me so often. I am very sorry for not answering you sooner but I have been very busy these last few days and was not much in the mood for writing letters.

I went in the day before yesterday to the town we are stationed near and drew pay and paid the wagon line returning in the afternoon in time to go up for night duty to the old slag heap. It was much better this time as we had a bucket of charcoal and made hot tea, into which for lack of milk we had put rum. We were all very sorry about this because of course none of us liked the rum but when you have no milk what are you to do? Yesterday I slept all morning to make up for last time. And even this morning my early rising was conspicuous only by its absence.

I wish you to not allude to my misspent year in a frivolous and irresponsible way. I, even if you are not, am heartily ashamed of the fact that I ever studied the language of the Hun, and whenever anyone speaks German he gets chairs and things thrown at his head so that it is better to pretend not to know it. The only occasion on which I spoke German was just after mounting the Major's horse to go in to the town as afore described. Waving my hand gaily I remarked "Auf Wiedersehen" and set spurs to my nag. I was far enough away to avoid pursuit by the time they had recovered from their surprise.

I have, during my leisure moments, made a practice of thinking out all the most insulting remarks I have ever learned in French, so that in case I have to tell off a little "gamin" I shall be well equipped. In the middle of my labours of doling out francs to tired drivers a little wretch came right into the office and said "Paipah Paipah." I turned round in the chair and let off a perfect flood of abuse which had the desirable effect of both turning the beggar out and earning the unbounded admiration of the men who were waiting to be paid. This shows you how good a thing it is to do a little extra work at anything. It will always come in handy.

I must admit however that my dignity was somewhat endangered by the fact that the monkey was always tiptoeing up to the window and shrieking "PAIPAH" and then running away as fast as he could much to the delight of the men. However these things will always happen.

Well, old girl, the best of luck and happiness not to mention success even in your unpalatable studies. I don't think you need fear ever becoming narrow-minded.

Your loving brother, Thornley

February 11th, 1916: Thornley to Molly

My dear Molly,

Thank you so much for your letter. I must apologise for exhorting you to keep the home fires burning, it must be a very sore subject with you. When I say keep the home fires burning I mean your fires, those that are of you and you alone, the fires of energy and enthusiasm, which side by side illuminate the altar of beauty and truth. These are the fires, O Vestal, which I exhort you in the stirring words of that noble anthem, to keep alight, not merely physical ones of the flesh. (Bouff! Bouff! Likewise pip! pip!)

The vision of you in your nightie looking for Zepps woke me up in the middle of last night and I spent about half an hour laughing. You have thus earned the enmity of the rats who were disturbed from their frolicsome employ and had to take cover.

Real army ration rum (which must be the real stuff) is, in spite of B.W. and her sherry, a dark claret red, which goes a beautiful colour when you dilute it.

According to your instructions, I sent the Bosches three salvos with your love. As there are four guns to a battery you will realise with your great mathematical capabilities that that makes a round dozen for a round Hun.

Well, cheeroh and keep the fires of your spirit* in good repair. Your loving brother, Thornley

*N.B. this has no reference to the rum mentioned above

February 13th, 1916: Thornley to Molly

My dearest Emma (N.B. Army parlance for M, your initial, I think).

Thank you so much for your letter. I am not sure whether I told you of the brilliant move I made to secure letters from our common brothers.

I wrote to J. and told him that I held him responsible for B. and unless a letter arrives soon from one of them every week I should make it known to the House. I mean to imply to the school that he, J. Woods, this great man the Senior whip, had to write home for P.M.[30] every week!!! In course of time my blackmail had effect and a letter arrived from both in which Jack said "I will try to write to you regularly though even thus I am afraid I cannot save my face. It is the most fertile

---

[30] Pocket money

skin I ever met!" Ha! (A Joak as Rowan said in his letter, it took me about two minutes to see the said JOAK but this by the way.) HA! Poor old spotty being.

They seem to have had Zepps over Shrewsbury also and there has been a lighting order in the School (so that they go tripping on their way down to prep in the evenings).

I was much amused by your description of Belgian Horticulture. My experience of French Horticulture is almost similar except that instead of filling the trenches you dig the Hun does it for you or else the rain comes along and snookers the thing up and it all begins to cave in. Il est drôle existence par ici!

Please don't go away with the idea that I pass cold nights every night. During my whole stay out here I have only had two bad ones. My own little cottage by the sea is an extremely commodious and large place where all the modem conveniences of space are combined with quiet air and absence of battles. All of which combined you will agree leave nothing further to be offered by life.

Well, I think there is very little else to say and so with kind thoughts, love and best wishes I will do what the men call "draw to a close."

Your loving brother, Thornley.

February 25th, 1916: Thornley to Molly

Thanks so much for your letter. I appreciate your position as a seconder both as a source of joy and as a source of panic to the full. I have been through it myself at a school debate.

That fire brigade is another rotten concern. The captain ought to be made to do the whole show herself. She must be a beast.

That lecture woman ought to come into the category of "prosy dull society sinners" over which the Mikado gloats. What punishment do you think would fit the case?

I am afraid I cannot give you any hints on the subject of your debate, the only ones I can think of at present are the most obvious ones, e.g.
1. Broadening of mental outlook.
2. In case of spinsterhood fitting a girl to support herself.
3. In public life it gives her the firm basis of confidence in herself (quite unnecessary, as far as I can see for most women) and in her views, which she has had plenty of time to think out for herself. Above all, don't read your speech - make notes to carry you through, but talk, don't read.

If you like I will write a letter to a chap I know at school and send it to you, you can then hold this over the commoners'[31] heads as I am doing and threaten to send it off if they do not write. What do you think?

I have no more time as the post leaves now. Your loving bro. Thor

---

[31] Jack and Bobby

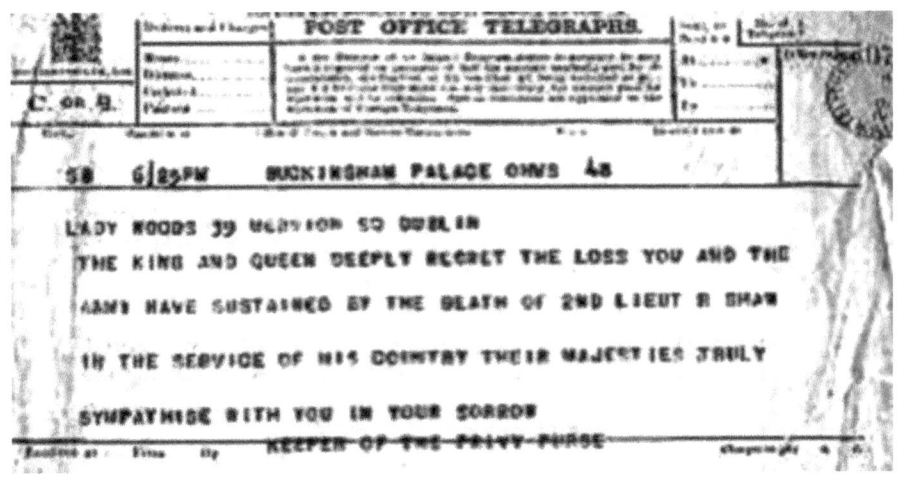

February 26th, 1916: Meg to Molly

My darling Molly

Our beloved Rowan has been killed – I had the telegram just now – on 23rd – no details. I know, my dearest, how you will feel it and my heart is aching for us all – God help us. He was so full of life and so gallant and brave, but he did the right thing and it was a glorious end. Forgive the scrawl. I can't write any more, it has been a bitter blow. Your loving Mother

February 27th, 1916: Meg to Molly

I have heard from Rowan's captain. He was out on patrol duty with a sergeant and two bombers and they saw a small party of Germans who suddenly disappeared. Rowan stood up to see where they had gone, and was shot instantly. There was snow on the ground and they were within 30 yards of the German trench, so they couldn't have missed him. He was killed instantaneously and they brought his body in. Captain Jackson wired to Billy, and they buried him behind the lines at Pont-du-Hem, between Estaires and La Bassée.

Don't grieve, I am trying not to – let us feel nothing but pride in his gallant

Lieut. Rowan Shaw Killed.

The death is announced of Lieut. Rowan Shaw, who was killed in Flanders in the early morning of February 23. The manner of his death, says the Times of Malaya, was as follows:—On the evening of February 22 he was asked to make a reconnaissance on the German trenches and select a place for the driving of a sap. He went out, carried out his duty, returned safely, and wrote a detailed account of the ground to his superiors. There, however, was some point on which he was not quite certain, and again about 3 a.m. on the 23rd he went out with a sergeant and two men towards the enemy trenches. This was gratuitous in a sense and only done from a high notion of duty. When within thirty yards of the enemy a German patrol appeared, making towards him, but it suddenly disappeared, and Lieut. Shaw jumped up on a sort of parapet in order to catch sight of it when he was hit by a sniper. He was at once carried back and was attended to by a doctor within five minutes, but it was found that he was dead. Death must have been instantaneous.

memory. I wanted you to know at once that he did not suffer. All the horrors were spared to him. He evidently was so keen about the bit of work that he forgot his own safety – it was like him, the dear brave fellow. Don't think about wearing black till you come home – thank goodness, soon now! I am trying to go on as usual and make no difference. There is so much grief in the world just now that we ought not to inflict our private sorrows on our friends. I am afraid my letter yesterday was very curt, but I was dazed with the shock. Forgive me for telling you like that, but it could not have been worse than opening the telegram.

Thank God, Thornley and Billy are safe – at least I hope so – but one never knows now. You'll be home in a little over a fortnight now, and it will be good to see you again. With loads of love, my darling. Your loving Mother

DD: *In 1899, after the outbreak of the Boer War, Rowan volunteered for service in South Africa in the Imperial Yeomanry. In the summer of 1900 he was involved in "the disaster at Lindley" and for some months he was a prisoner and was released. He became a solicitor and went to the Malay States in October 1908.*

March 11th, 1916: Thornley to Molly

My Dearest Molly,

Thank you very much indeed for your letter. I know of course how hard it is to write letters to Mother now but I try to be cheerful and not to mention Rowan in them when I write.

By Jove just to think of you going home in a fortnight. I don't suppose I shall see the shores of La Belle France receding for another six or seven months, though with luck I might be home in 4 or 5. Still it is not all that bad out here. My present work is interesting enough and my quarters are comfortable.

A six inch Hun shell plunked straight into the mess room of the battery next to me in our old position. I used to go and have tea there often enough before another lot took over. It killed two servants and permanently disabled another. The only officer who was in at the time was buried and had a very bad shake-up – he has been sent home. So together they got off very luckily.

There is little enough news just now, keep going and cheer up. This show is going to be over much sooner than people think and when I march through London on the right hand side of Sir Douglas Haig you can get in one of Betty's windows and scream. Your loving brother, Thor.

March 3rd, 1916: Thornley to Meg

My dearest Mother

Thank you very much indeed for: (1) the boots and gaiters; (2) The Spectator; and (3) The parcel from Findlater's. The last was a great success, the chocolates and sweets were very good and the coffee was excellent.

The weather out here has been bad lately, snow sometimes and frost at nights and until I got my shelters put up in the face of tremendous odds in the way of lack of material - my poor horses had a wretched time of it.

They are however in very good condition now and I am getting my lines into proper condition. The General and the Staff Captain came round this evening just as the men were knocking off and the Gen. was greatly bucked and said so.

By dint of pointing out to about six local rustics how useful the muck from our lines would be to them, I have got them racing one another to take it away, all trying to get into it before the others get there. By this simple stratagem I conciliate: a. the rustics; b. the general; and c. the men, who have so much the less dirty labour.

I got the deuce of a toss off the mare I was riding today in front of all the men.

I had made them take up their stirrups and was jogging along in front of the exercise when I saw a man cantering a pair of horses along the road H.B.

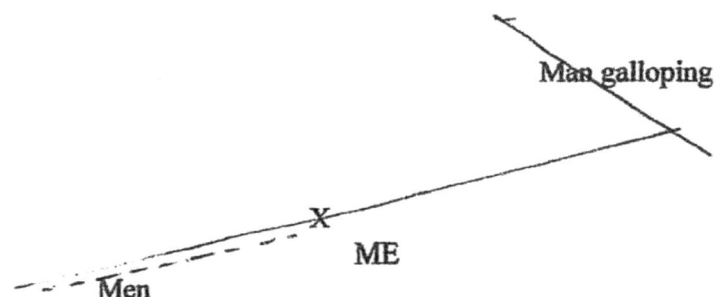

I put the horse into the field on the left and started cantering over to intercept him (you know how easy it is to sit on a horse cantering) and was careless as to my seat, when the mare shied across to the right and I stayed where I was for a moment, then I came down. I was not in the least hurt, and hardly even shaken, so to I show that I was not such a poor horseman as they supposed.

I trotted them round without stirrups till only myself and the 3 N.C.O.s were left without holding the saddle. I had great fun with the old wheeze hurled so often at my head in the riding school, "I can guarantee the saddle, driver Davies – it won't come off – you needn't hold it on." etc. Vindictive spirit – you say – well, perhaps, but only human.

I am very busy down here at present – that is to say, pleasantly busy without being overworked. The only thing that tries my nerves is when the padre comes round on Saturdays and wants a large turnout for Church Parade the following morning and hints more than broadly that it is about time that I myself put in an appearance. I think I shall go tomorrow, not because of the padre – I'm afraid it will only encourage him – but because of the men. I have had the maxim rubbed into me "Never ask a man to do dirty work which you are not prepared to do yourself." Well, goodbye and cheer up, Mother, I don't know when I will get leave, in another 4 or 5 months perhaps if I am lucky.

Your loving Son, Thornley S. Woods

March 11th, 1916: Billy to Molly

My dear Molly

Thank you very much for both your letters. We had only been in reserve for about ten days when we were marched right down here to take over a bit of the line from the French. We have all to live in dug-outs as there are not billets in the place at all. I imagine Thornley is somewhere near me along this line and I am going to try to find out where he is. There is a lot of snow lying about but I hope it will soon go and the spring will come. I had a letter from your Mother a short while ago. I'm afraid she is feeling Rowan's loss terribly as indeed we all do. I suppose you will soon be going home again from Cambridge. I will write again as soon as I get settled down. Ever your loving uncle, Billy

March 19th, 1916: Thornley to Molly

I expect that you are home by now and anyhow will be by the time you get this. I am writing it from our O.P., which is situated in an old communications trench only used now by us and commanding a good view over the front line trenches; so you will be able to see that I have returned from the wagon line. We are in action in a street of little workmen's cottages, all very well built and each possessing a very commodious shellproof cellar.

The house above sets the shell off and the cellar itself stops the splinters coming through. The whole place is in ruins as it had to stand a good deal of fire, but the Hun hardly ever fires at it now, so we live a life of ease.

Things are very quiet up here with an odd shell going off over at the trenches and I am at present sitting outside in the sun writing this. The weather for the last few days has been splendid – just like summer and we are really having a very easy time.

I had a letter from each of the scions of our noble house at Shrewsbury, both of whom seem to be looking forward to the holidays. Bobby seems to have had a touch of 'flu and to be feeling the worse for wear but John, the recreant writer, seems to be flourishing like the green bay tree. In fact one might almost call him the "curious bay."

It is perhaps just as well that I left the wagon line when I did. The policy of building, though an excellent one, has many attendant discomforts and when one is furnished with a "miserapolous" Lieut-Major who pinches what he can't get from the government, the moment comes sooner or later when one is "wanted" in several quarters. I have taken to my heels and left the aforesaid L.-M. to bear a want (?) whose load I am convinced will not be beyond his power of endurance. In fact I only wish I could be there as a disinterested spectator of a scene which will be amusing in the extreme, but as things stand I am content with my little cellar (No. 18 Park Lane) and obscurity.

The great point about trenches old or new is that the Hun has as much chance of distinguishing you from your surroundings as of coming over to have a look at you. I have just been trying to scrape about two thirds of LA BELLE FRANCE off my boots and have succeeded in getting about one third off. I incontinently stepped on the scrapings and am now as bad as ever. Anyhow, here's to the man who invented gumboots, and to the woman who knits me socks, but especially to the latter.

I am writing a considerable percentage of rot - of that I am quite aware - but I am have finished my book and am waiting to be relieved for lunch so must fill my time in somehow.

The scene is very peaceful, the birds are twittering, the aeroplanes are humming, the sun is shining and the Hun is "pooping" (only an occasional Whizzbang) and I am comfortable. What in fact has life further to offer? Only the appearance of the relieving observer and lunch.

I had a rather beastly experience before I came up here. We had to shoot a poor old mare who was getting worse and worse of a disease contracted some time ago. The Veterinary Corps Sergeant attached to us did the deed, and did it well, but the piteous look on the old girl's face rather turned me. I am glad I didn't know her very well but it was bad enough as it was.

It is now 12.58 so that blighter should be turning up any minute now. I find that after my fortnight at the W.L.[32] these battery people are inclined to look down on me as a "back of the front hover coper" and I have been at pains to point out to them that without me they would have had no food or supplies and would have degenerated into "front of the front rat eaters," but they don't see my point of view.

Sniper's bullet just passed overhead but as I can't put my head over the trench without a ladder and am at present sitting down, little things like that don't worry me much. I suppose he got a letter from home and was loosing off in an excess of increasing joy. Nothing much doing, all very quiet. I will close this letter with my best love to all and an empty belly. Sorry it is so short, I will write a longer one next time. Your loving brother, Thornley

March 29th, 1916: Thornley to Molly

My dearest Molly,

Thank you very much for your letter which I received last night. It is very good of you to write so often.

The workman's cottage in whose cellar I find myself is one of the ruins of a model village, built by the proprietor of a mine close at hand for the benefit of the employees. It must have been a very comfy place before it got knocked down.

---

[32] Wagon Line

I'm glad I shall get my watch soon. I have been feeling the need of same very much since I sent it away to you. I'll take the chance of the other one being worn out. I don't think the war will last as long as that.

I am sorry you are having trouble with a toD. (This looks like saying TOOTH with all A.W.W.B.'s fingers on the article in question) but we will hope for the best. As regards what you say about note paper. I always write on both sides of what Mother supplies. This is Army paper and is supplied free, I therefore write on one side only. And talking about paper I am nearly through the last lot of envelopes although there is some paper to be used. I will steal some envelopes and let you know when I want another block.

I am glad Mother is better. I am sure that by the time the war is over she will be able to take part in the general rejoicings with as much spirit as any of us. By the way this may seem callous but as the war is going to come to an end on April 17th 1916 it is rather better than it sounds.

You will notice by this paper that I'm writing you a letter in the O.P., it is a very fine morning but the wind is rather cold so I am writing inside. I tried to sit outside but failed even when muffled up.

Life goes on in much the same way out here, we are drudging along in the same old way with just enough to interest us and not enough to excite us.

Members of the battery are talking about a move in spring but they don't believe the war will finish by 17th April. I smile. My superior knowledge enables me to regard their vile anticipations more in the light of a joke than an effort to make my blood run cold.

It appears that all my labour (carting trees and sandbags and things all over the countryside to make gun pits) has been in vain. Our orders are to hold on until we get further orders and in the meanwhile the stuff I dumped is being rapidly demolished by the infantry in the way of firewood. Horrid way these blighters have of ordering you to do a thing and just after the most awful exertions and stupendous amount of nagging of supply officers you get the thing really well in hand, they say "Oh, no, I'm not sure about that. I don't think I'll have it done after all, anyhow don't do anything more till you hear from us."

While it is an interesting thing to see ways and means in an apparently hopeless task to do, if I am set down to draw more stuff I will repair a light railway, bag some trolley wheels I saw nearby and do the carting from the road to the position in the proper style.

I don't think there is much more to say, as in fact I have been writing this against time, trying to hold out until the man who relieves me arrives. I am afraid it is no good however and I will have to return to a magic book of Masefield's called "Multitude and Solitude[33]". I wonder if you have read it?

There is absolutely nothing doing out of the window. I can't see any movement at all in the Hun front line trench and very little indeed in ours.

---

[33] John Masefield *Multitude and Solitude* (1909)

Personally I don't think there are any Huns in front of us at all. Perhaps a couple to shoot machine guns, etc. but nothing to speak of. Your loving brother, Thornley. P.S. Love to all at home.

March 31st, 1916: Thornley to Molly

Thanks muchly for your letter. Its opening puts one in mind of the French exercise book written by my old pal Henri Bue (or Henry Boo as we used to call him). "I have not been to church but I have bagged a writing pad" -"Has your aunt got a motor car?" "No, but my cousin (female) has a fast pig." "Ta tante a-t-elle une automobile?" - "Non, mais ma cousine a une porc rapide," or words to that effect. You will excuse this witty strain when you realise that I am just back from night duty, and am now shaved, washed, oiled and curled. On the way back I was not hit by a shell but the little buzzy bits came a lot too close for yours truly who made himself scarce as soon as dignity and a pair of insecure knees permitted.

I got the parcel of cake and sweets and watch and paper. My dear, thank you mille fois for your kindness. Of course I showed the box of sweets to the mess in general and then shut it up quickly and put it away because it was breakfast and one shouldn't eat sweets at breakfast; so they all ran outside and behaved like a German band looking at lemons. (I will draw a veil over the undignified scene.)

The weather out here has been heavenly for the last two or three days. We had a lovely bit about 10 days ago and then more snow but now it is beatific again.

Don't laugh when you hear this - I have just adopted a cat. She lives among the ruins here and sleeps in my cellar and catches my mice and kills my rats and in general makes herself useful. I adopted a mongrel cur too but that was too much company and the mongrel cur always had the worst of it so with great tact and delicacy withdrew and I have not seen him for about a week.

Thanks for the offer of "litrachat." I am at present in the throes of a book by John Masefield called "Multitude and Solitude." It is written as a novel but it is really a study on the question of art and learning and its place in the world. The Major has two books by William le Queux[34] sent out every week which he devours with glee, but they are not for me, his genius is too great for my poor spirit. I should very much like you to send me out a couple of decent novels now and then. Life out here is the same as ever. I have not been across to my gun pits since I wrote last, and I hope the stuff is not all bagged by now, but I expect it is. We have really got settled in comfortably now and everything is going O.K. There was an awful lot of work to be done on the bally place when we came but it is all straight now.

Thank you very much again for the parcel and thank Mother from me. Tell her I will write to her soon. Your loving bro. Thornley

---

[34] William Le Queux (1864-1927), a popular Anglo-French journalist and mystery, thriller and espionage writer.

April 17th, 1916: Thornley to Molly

Thank you very much indeed for your letter, I was much amused at the picture of Robert mending the engine.

I am afraid there is no earthly hope of my getting any leave yet awhile. It is a nuisance as I should have seen you all if I had come home now but maybe I shall get it during the summer hols and that will be better fun.

All sorts of rumours are current as to what we shall do (by that I do not mean the British army, but A162 R.F.A.) in the immediate future, I think we shall probably go join to rest as it is about 8 months since the brigade was out of the firing line. I can't say I care much either it's at present a case of "peace perfect peace our future all unknown!" [35]

This course I am on is simply hair-raising balderdash. They treat you as if you had never seen an 18 pounder, and then, they irony of fate, they started showing me how to build gun-pits. That was the last edge or I thought it was, as I have been doing nothing else for the last four months. But worse was to come. They took us up to a battery position and settled us down in someone else's badly built gun pit to watch a subaltern testing sights, a young idiot that had been out about a fortnight and knew sweet Fanny Adams about the whole show. I may mention now that sight testing is done daily in A162 and I have to do both my guns. That is to say, taking it that I have been out here 3½ months that I have tested sights 204 times since I have been out. It makes me howl.

Of course there are some really good moments. We have an awfully interesting man who lectures on telephones and this afternoon they told us something about the 4.5 How. In fact when anyone else is in charge except that hair-entangling lost sheep of a self-satisfied idiot Colonel man who is in charge, everything goes well, but we are sadly left to ourselves, as Mother would say, when we fall into his clutches.

Please thank Mother for the parcel from Findlater and for the papers, I enjoyed same very much indeed, thanks.

I am afraid I cannot write a separate letter to her as we are kept pretty busy being informed that we are young officers and that our ignorance is something to shudder at.

As a marginal not anybody who wants to be particularly offensive to us calls us young officers, and although we are young - and officers - there is something so confoundedly patronising in the term that it is like a red rag to a bull when anyone uses it of me now. I often think how awful the naked truth can be!

No more news so will dry up.

Love to all. Your exasperated bro. Thornley.

---

[35] From a hymn by Edward H. Bickersteth, Jr., 1875, inspired by Isaiah 26:3.

Chapter III

Dublin Easter Rising
First-hand account from Molly Woods

Molly Woods, who was prevented by the Easter Rising of April 24th, 1916, from returning to Cambridge, started a day by day account of the dreadful situation around Merrion Square, etc. which she eventually posted to her brother Thornley in France. Her whole family, which included the two schoolboys, played their part in the rescue of the wounded and the improvised help the local doctors arranged for them at No. 40 Merrion Square. For this she received a bronze medal from the St. John's Ambulance Brigade.

The Woods family, like many others in Dublin, spent Easter Monday at their country retreat. This was "Rathleigh", on the slope of Killiney Hill, with a fine view of Bray Head from the garden. They returned in the evening to find the streets of Dublin deserted.

May 2nd, 1916: Molly to Thornley
39 Merrion Square

Dearest Thor,

There is at last time to write and tell you all that happened and I know you must be pining for news of the appalling doings in your native land. I will begin at the beginning and tell you exactly what happened from our point of view. It may be a few days yet before we can get letters through.

On Easter Monday we put our lunch up and went on one of our rare excursions to Rathleigh (rare on account of the scarcity of petrol) and having had a very pleasant day we came home about 3.30 p.m. When we reached Temple Hill our attention was attracted by an excited crowd of 20 or 30 tram men outside the tram sheds and by the fact that the sheds were full of trams.

We thought there was a strike on and drove on into town not seeing a single tram on the way, but groups of people waiting for them everywhere. As we were driving along Northumberland Road I noticed that the windows of the Parochial Hall (a small red building on the left) were barricaded with mattresses and sacks. We did not think much of it at the time but drove on into the stable the car being laden with empty bottles for the purpose ye wot [sic]. We came through the house and were informed by Lloyd[36] that the "Volunteers" had had a row with the military. I had better explain at once that considerable confusion has arisen in people's minds about these volunteers. They are not the National Volunteers who have been loyal all along and who have helped the government, but the Irish Volunteers or as we prefer to call them the Sinn Fein Volunteers. (Pron. Thin Fain in case you have forgotten!) Coupled with them you get the Citizen Army. The organiser is Connolly Larkin's brother-in-law for whom I have nothing to say; but the rank and file believe they are doing the best for their country, and most of them are patriots and in the highest state of mental exaltation. They have been made a catspaw by Germany. They have been misled and deserve your pity. However to my narrative.

We came through the house on to the doorstep where we found that most of the neighbours were also on their doorsteps and everybody was standing in groups and talking. Daddy said he would walk up to the Club and see if he could get some news and started off. Mother went down to the corner to talk to Mrs Finny and Lady Myles. We stood on the doorstep and heard occasional shots in the distance. Presently Mother came back with the news that Mrs. Finny had seen the Sinn Feiners march fully armed into Dublin shortly after we had left and that

---

[36] Lloyd was Sir Robert's butler, who had fought in the Zulu war. He frightened the maids by telling them that the Germans would come swarming up Killiney beach with feathers on their heads waving their assegais!

they had taken possession of the G.P.O., The Castle, Westland Row, Liberty Hall, etc and had proclaimed an Irish Republic.

All these places had been thrown into a state of defence also which alarmed us greatly that they had entrenched themselves in Stephen's Green and that the fighting was very hot round there. The direction from which we heard the shots confirmed this. Dr. Daly had been in the University Club early in the afternoon and a bullet aimed at him from the Green (by the Countess Markievicz[37] as we afterwards heard) had missed his head by about three inches. Mother at once got into a fearful state of anxiety about Daddy which was not relieved by the fact that when we rang up we were told he had not arrived at the Club. (I forgot to say that the Sinn Feiners had cut all the telegraph wires and cables at the post offices and all communication to England (except by wireless from Kingstown) was cut off. The trams had been stopped by the Sinn Feiners who held the power house. After being for some time in considerable suspense about Daddy he came back having been unable to get through to the Club but having heard a good deal of news. A great many people had been shot. Soldiers by design, civilians generally by accident. The rebels had the College of Surgeons and Jacob's Biscuit Factory. We rang up the Alton's. Mr. A. had gone down to Trinity, and as most of the people were away, was at the head of a band of about 20 O.T.C's[38], and was organizing the defence. We were in a great state of excitement and were having tea (with Mr. Hewett) in the drawing room, when a G.R. in mufti luckily for him came to Dr. Beatty from Beggar's Bush Barracks to say they had a casualty there and Dr. Beatty was the first Doctor he had found at home. Dr. B. came for Daddy and they commandeered a motor car which had just driven up to 32 [Merrion Square] and drove to Sir P. Dun's to get dressings. When they reached Sir P. Dun's they found the rebels had got Boland's Bakery immediately opposite. The windows were barricaded with sacks of flour and the rifles were pointing out commanding the whole street and the hospital. Daddy etc did not like the look of this so they improvised a large Red Cross out of a red blanket some white lint and rubber plaster and stuck it on the wind screen. They went on without being molested, however, but when they reached Haddington Road and were about to turn the corner the people shouted "Don't go there, you'll be shot." The shover[39] got into a funk and said he would not go on.

The G.R. who was sitting in front gave him a piece of his mind and he went on. They saw that the Sinn Feiners had possession of the railway bridge and were commanding the whole road in front of Beggar's Bush. If you remember it goes like this.

---

[37] Constance Georgine Markievicz, née Gore-Booth 1868 – 1927 Sinn Fein and Fianna Fail politician.
[38] See Chapter V
[39] chauffeur

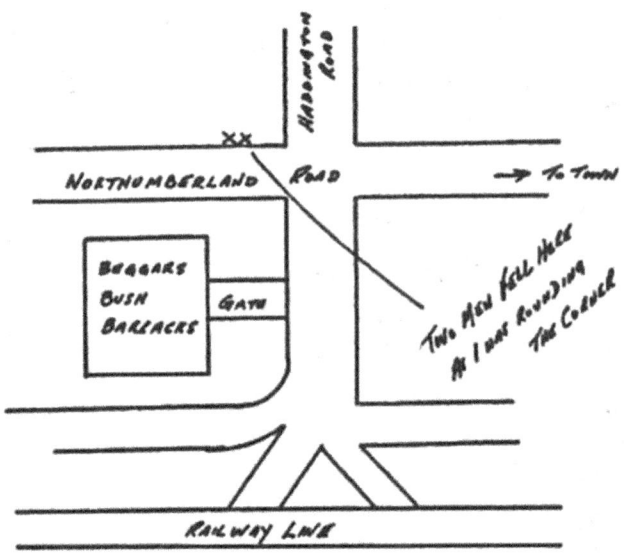

They were behind sand bags on the bridge. They rushed up to the barracks gate and at first the G.R.s who were holding it did not want to let them in as they were not in uniform; at last, however, they did and as soon as they went in the cowardly motorman did a bunk with the car and left them there.

If they had not had the Red Cross they would probably have been fired on when they were seen going into the barracks. Daddy attended the man who was very bad and in fact died later on and they telephoned for an ambulance. It came and as it reached the door a bullet aimed at a soldier hit a man near the gate. The ambulance took him away and came back for the other. Daddy and Dr. Beatty escaped from Beggar's Bush in the Ambulance and took the man to hospital. They came home again and we spent the rest of the evening hanging about the doorstep and the balcony listening to the sounds of distant shots. Everything was fairly quiet when we were going to bed but as you can guess we did not get much sleep. About one o'clock Patsey came in to me in a fright and when I went to the front windows we heard a terrific fusillade going on in the direction of town. We have since learnt to gauge the firing and know now that this was not as bad as we had it later because each report in the streets produces half a dozen echoes; and a certain Capt. M. de B. Daly, who figures in this narrative later on, informed us that the sound of musketry in the streets is many times louder than in what you might call the open air. I am glad we were worked up to it gradually as it was quite terrifying enough to hear such sounds at dead of night in our hitherto peaceful city. We got to sleep again about 2 and at 5 Jack came in to tell me that the soldiers had arrived. (Up till then there had been no serious opposition to the rebels.) I went to the school-room windows and Lower Fitzwilliam Street had two companies (so Jack says) drawn up on both sides.

They had come up from the Curragh and had marched in from the direction of town, I don't yet know how they managed to do it without falling across the rebels somewhere else in town. It was dreadfully uncanny to see them sending out scouts and sentries to all the street corners and to see them going along doubled up and peering round the corner as if they expected to find almost anything in the next street. There was firing from the direction of Stephen's Green and the sound of a machine gun. We were not sure of this at the time but we have had reason since then to know the creatures better and it was one. After a while during which they sat and lay on the pavement, they marched down Baggot Street towards Stephen's Green in column; very shortly they came back and marched past the house and back again the way they came (7.30 a.m.) I do not think they had been fighting as they were too quick and the rebels retained possession of the Green. On Tuesday morning after breakfast Daddy, Mother, Jack and I ventured into town as far as Findlater's to try and procure food. Nearly all the shops were shut and finally we succeeded in getting some at Guingan's (the pub round the corner in Mount Street.) Daddy visited Elpis[40] in safety and then a couple of shots of startling proximity moved everyone along and us indoors. I should mention that the police were confined to barracks during the whole business as they had no arms; that there was not the slightest panic or fear among the people; that everybody was quiet and the place was like a Sunday except that there was no traffic. Nothing happened near us on Tuesday but all day long there was considerable firing from Sackville Street[41], Stephen's Green and Boland's.

We hung about on the steps and at the windows and heard all possible rumours true and untrue, possible and impossible. Some rain fell in the afternoon but otherwise the weather was perfect.

In fact it was so quiet in the morning that we began to think all was over but in the evening we heard the first of the bombarding. The heavy guns were hammering away someplace in the city. (Sackville Street as you shall see.) Tuesday night we are all a little hazy about as we were all very tired after the night before and slept like logs. On Wednesday morning there was a great rush of people to buy bread from the carts which drew up in the streets in front of the house and people were seen carrying numbers of loaves going in all directions. On Wednesday morning also though we did not know at the time the soldiers landed at Kingstown and started to march into Dublin. And as we afterwards heard the officer who was temporarily attached to them (Sherwood Foresters) as a guide was Capt. M. de B. Daly of whom you may have heard. There had been fighting at intervals all the time in front of Beggar's Bash as the Sinn Feiners were anxious

---

[40] Miss Huxley's Nursing Home.
[41] Present day O'Connell Street.

to take it and the G.R.s were equally anxious that they shouldn't. The soldiers reached Carisbrooke House (between Pembroke and Northumberland Roads) and passed it and then the second lot marching along got fired on from Prof. Metham's House (which had been commandeered) in the Botanical Gardens.

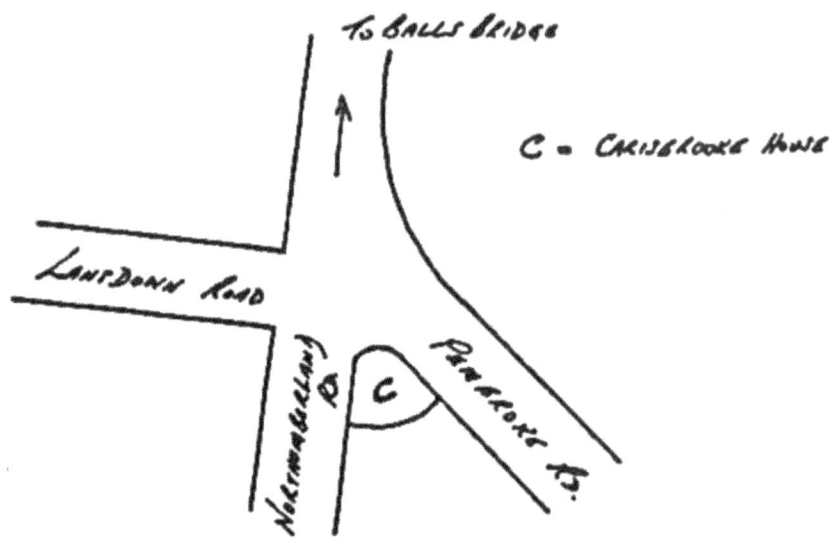

This all we heard from Ulick afterwards. Then they had an awful time at Carisbrooke House which however did not last long and the Sinn Fein defenders were killed. The first lot, however, had passed and fell into the trap which had been laid for them. When they reached Haddington Road there was a fierce battle as the Sinn Feiners had the two corner houses and the soldiers had come without a bomb or a gun of any kind and the commander tried to rush the houses. The disposition was this.

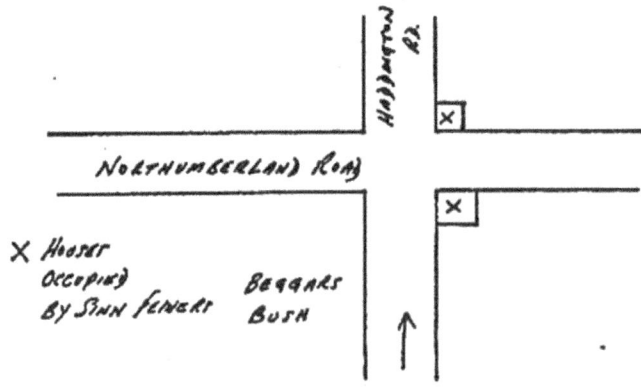

The arrow shows the direction of the cross fire from the railway bridge shown in the first map I drew. I forgot to say the rebels held the whole railway line from Amiens St. to Lansdown Road including Tara Street Station, Westland Row and the Custom House. There was a fierce battle here but they eventually fought their way down Haddington Road being sniped at from the houses on both sides and from the Parochial Hall (above mentioned). They reached Mount Street Bridge where the most serious resistance of all was offered them. The heaviest fighting and the largest number of casualties took place here. You can imagine what all this sounded like at 39. We walked to the corner and peeped round. From here we saw a good deal of what was going on and were fairly safe as there was a huge crowd drawn up in Mount Street, watching the battle exactly as if it had been a football match, and they stopped the stray bullets. The people were perfectly indifferent and reckless. Later on however when the bullets began to come down the street we cleared away.

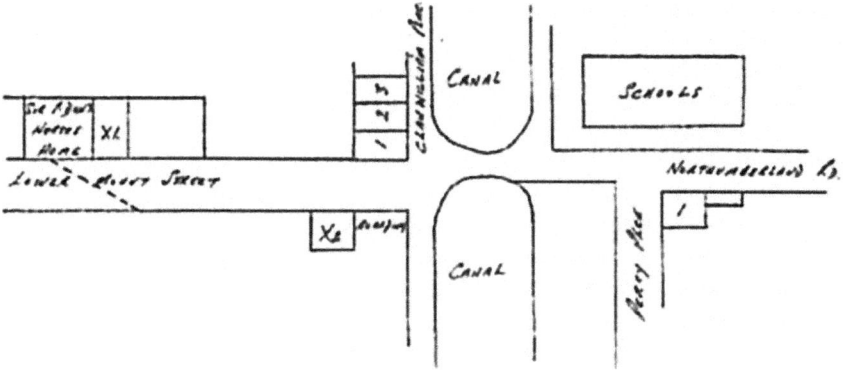

The rebels held 1 and 2 Clanwilliam Place which command Northumberland Road. They held the schools, 1. Percy Place and the houses marked X in Mount Street. The crowd was drawn up diagonally across the street in front of the Nurses Home watching a sniper in the house next door.

The soldiers took and held 1 Percy Place. They tried to rush the schools and they tried to rush the Clanwilliam Houses but of course it was useless the whole bottom story was barricaded. They were a 3rd line territorial regiment with 6 – 10 weeks training who had never fired anything but blanks (so Ulick says but he is not sure about the last). The Sinn Feiners luckily were equally bad shots but they had a couple of good snipers posted round the place.

From 4 till 7 p.m. a furious and useless battle raged and we at the corner listened to the firing and watched the puffs of smoke from the rifle of the sniper in XI. Sir P. Dun's nurses showed the utmost intrepidity, dashing with stretchers into the middle of the hottest fighting under fire from both sides to carry the wounded soldiers into their home. We could see them running down the steps and Ulick said he had never seen anything finer.

At 7 o'clock a series of terrific explosions began and we thought they had brought up a gun. As a fact Ulick had got a lot of bombs from a friend of his and they were bombing out the schools. When they finished that a man crawled to the door of 1 Clanwilliam Place tied about 5 lbs of gun cotton to the handle and 10 secs later the Hall door was blown through the back of the house. They then rushed the house and took it putting a bomb into each room before they entered it. I know you well enough to know that you are subtracting a good deal from this account to allow for the fact that my recent acquaintance with war has caused me to exaggerate, but you will be startled into a sense of its moderation when you hear that the casualties on Mount Street Bridge on Wednesday afternoon were 19 officers and 200 men; and this I have from Ulick Daly who was there and saw it all. The Hospital of course could not accommodate all these so they turned the nurses' home into one and put the men into the nurses' beds, on mattresses on the floor and anything they could get, but many had nothing at all. Daddy was there till after twelve looking after the men and when we visited the corner at about 10.30 p.m. everything was very quiet and there was a great fire in Clanwilliam place. No. 1 and No. 2 were burnt out and the roofs fell in; I have since seen the place and the houses are gutted. The road and pavements over the bridge are discoloured with blood and the houses where the fighting was are wrecked and riddled with bullet holes.

From 10 p.m. on Wednesday till 4 a.m. on Thursday there was a blessed interval of quiet during which we all slept but at 4 o'clock when day came again the fighting advanced up Mount Street. Thursday and Friday were the two hottest days as far as we were concerned though of course Mount Street was the worst fighting. Between 5 and 6 they began firing down Grattan Street and round Boland's and the noise was so terrific and alarming (I had not been hardened then as I was later) that I left my room and went and sat in the bays window in front. The soldiers had reached the corner and had taken command of the side of the Square. They had sentries everywhere and when I put my head out of the window I had a gun pointed at me. I took it in with great rapidity! The soldiers searched the Square and beat all the bushes for rebels. Here is the disposition of the forces.

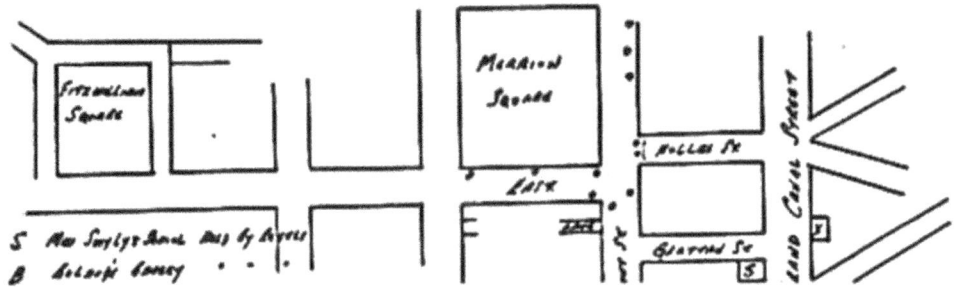

While Bobby was dressing he hung out of the window to have a look and, something fell on his head. This turned out to be a chip knocked off the chimney by a bullet. Bobby was greatly astonished.

Just after breakfast Mrs. Lumsden who had been sending off supplies of dressings from the depot next door came in and asked us if we would make some Red Cross armlets for the ambulance men as they had not enough, so we went in next door and machined furiously all morning. About twelve o'clock an urgent request came for field dressings and we began to make them; about 12.30 Dr. Ella Webb arrived and asked if we could put down some mattresses in the empty rooms to take some of the men as they were fighting in Grattan Street and Mount Boland's. We turned to and worked as none of us had ever worked before or since. We beat up mattresses and all the requirements for a hospital round the Square and three hours later we had 14 cases in and an operation was being done in a theatre which had not existed 2 hours previously. When I say we I mean a great many people connected with the depot and all the V.A.Ds they could beat up. We unskilled people, that is unskilled in nursing, had an urgent message sent up to us for dressings and from 5-7 we made them furiously. The ambulance kept on arriving and by evening we had 24 cases in, most of them soldiers but several civilians and one poor small boy. Jack did splendid work. He and another man carried the stretchers up and down stairs all afternoon and carried some of the men up the street to the Red Cross depot in Fitzwilliam Street where they had started another hospital. We sent them the slight cases. In the meantime the soldiers had barricaded Holles Street and there was sniping going on both there and in Mount Street, besides fighting going on all over different parts of town. About 7.30 they asked me to go and borrow some boracic powder off Miss Huxley as they had none, and as I could not, of course, go by Mount Street as there were snipers on every second roof, I went by the back lane. I had just reached Mrs Huxley's back gate when some of my friends of the Babies Club rushed out and dragged me into one of the little houses, pointing out a sniper on the roof of one of the Merrion Square houses between ours and the corner. As I daresay you are aware, your sister is far from valiant and though morally convinced that the man would not fire at me, I was in a mortal funk. One of the natives went across the lane and kicked Miss Huxley's back gate until she opened it, very cautiously, asking for credentials as she did so. I dashed across and threw myself into her arms. I had better mention here in justice to the Sinn Feiners that though you may call them rebels, lunatics and murderers and disturbers of the peace or any other name you can think of, the large majority of them have done what the soldiers call "fought clean." Of course you will hear awful stories of what they did, and I grant you their ammunition was dirty - but they did not fire on the Red Cross as some people have tried to make out.

I had taken my cap and apron off and was in ordinary civilian attire and I was equally safe in either. I got the powder from Miss H. thanked my friends at the cottage, and came back keeping well under cover of the wall. I was strongly tempted to run, if the truth must be told it was all I could do not to run, but I succeeded in walking back and up the garden and delivering the boric powder next door, without a stain on my character.

On Thursday night there were two terrific fires is the city. Sackville Street had been bombarded with 18 pounder guns during the afternoon and the whole of the right hand (east side) was razed. I have since seen it and it is wicked, the fire burnt for 5 days and they started on the other side next day. You have looked your last on one of the handsomest streets in Europe and I find it very hard to believe that so much wanton destruction was necessary.

The street is deep in heaps of smashed masonry. For 56 yards back from what was the street, there is a heap of smoking ruins with occasionally a high, charred wall sticking up. Such a scene of destruction and desolation I have never behold. The damage is estimated at 2 million pounds worth and we mourn in vain for our beautiful city. Henry Street is the same and in some places the street is 6 and 7 feet above the right level with bricks and rubble. The G.P.O. is gutted and nothing but the shell is left standing.

On Friday morning at sunrise (3 a.m.) a fusillade began in Grattan Street and the back lane, which by then was barricaded and machine guns and rifles rattled incessantly all morning. By then I had got used to them and slept whenever possible and we all rose early. The back of the house was hit a few times but each time on the masonry, and we were forced to evacuate the breakfast room. At 8 O'clock the fun began in front when a sniper in Holles Street dropped one of the soldiers at the barricade, and Dr. Crichton, who is staying with the Finny's and who is a big man, dashed out and carried him bodily into the hospital in 40. Luckily I went in next door fairly early as a little later two snipers were located, one on the end house of the south side and one half way up our side.

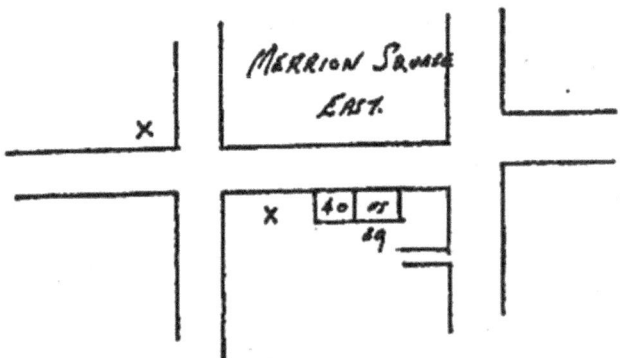

We had a soldier firing off our door step and the bullets were splashing about all up and down the street. I was upstairs in the workroom, superintending about 12 V.A.Ds who were making dressings, when an excited messenger came dashing upstairs asking for a Red Cross flag, in the name of the Lord to hang out in front or we'd be having the bullets in at the front windows. I rushed to the store room (luckily the depot had a huge supply of raw material) and we soon had a white sheet, but there was not a bit of anything red, we had used it all the day before. Miss Finny volunteered to go to their house for some she had but was not allowed to leave the house.

I bethought me of an old red table cloth in the school room and I dashed around to our house and Mother gave me some red turkey she happened to have. I got back with it in safety and started to make the flag with the people praying me to hurry. I worked that sewing machine with a prayer on my lips and a pain in my heart as I never worked any machine before and hope I never will again.

The flag was made and hung out and the battle ended and one of the snipers at least cleared away. I ought to mention here that the great difficulty with these rebels has been the facility with which they shinned along the roofs and got down through the skylights of empty or shut houses. The soldiers were quite ignorant of the geography of the city and of the principle on which these houses are built and they would not take advice from the people who knew. Consequently the rounding up of the snipers has been an eternal and quite unsuccessful job. The gallant Sharlott saw a man with a rifle come out of the back of a Mount Street house, put the rifle into hiding and sauntering out of the lane with his hands in his pockets, mingle with the crowd which was watching the soldiers firing up at the house he had just left! What did Sharlott do? You ought to know that Sharlott isn't the man to interfere with anyone who had a gun in his possession even if it was half a street away.

But to continue. We had a pretty warmish day all day on Friday with the bullets whistling about on all sides and the endless work to be done next door. We made dressings and we made armlets and during the afternoon I made 6 Red Cross flags for the motor cars to carry when working for us. Jack confessed he had never done a real day's work in his life before and I am inclined to agree, but at the same time you can imagine the blessing it was to have something to do after the oppressive idleness of the first two days.

On Saturday the soldiers got onto the roofs of the houses at the corner and the snipers got onto the backs of the Upper Mount Street houses and there was a great tattoo across the roofs of the little houses at the back. They thought there were Sinn Feiners in the basement of Dr. Dempsey's house at the corner so they bombed out the poor man's house and then mounted a Lewis gun on the roof and started giving the people in Upper Mount Street a horrible time. We could see the puffs of smoke replying to their fire from Upper Mount Street but needless to remark they did no harm to the snipers but killed and wounded innocent people who were doing no harm to anyone but who were luckless enough to live in Mount Street. The snipers just walked out whenever they pleased.

The sniping went on all day all round us and we toiled incessantly next door and in the afternoon the rumour reached us that the G.P.O. had surrendered.

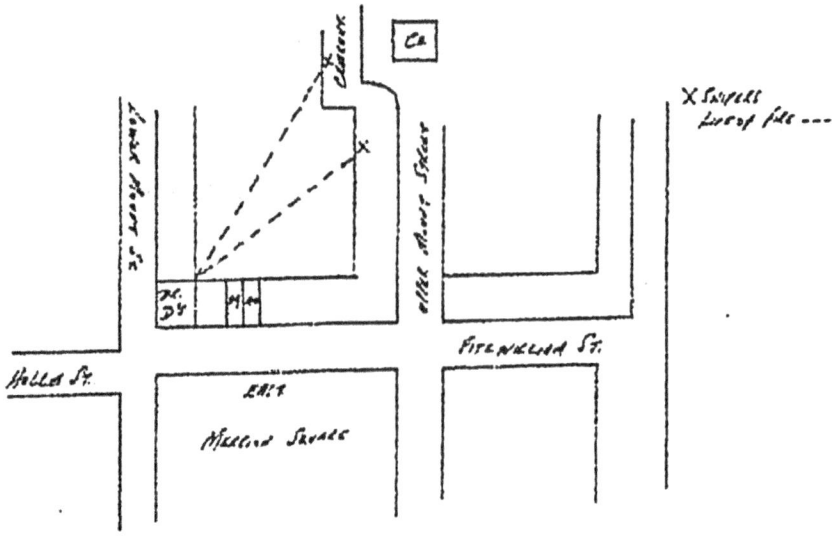

This seemed too good to be true, and we made a point of not believing it, but as it turned out it was true. The firing went on as before round us, however, as the isolated snipers were still holding out and the rebels retained possession of Boland's. Sunday, which is usually a day of rest and gladness was quite undistinguishable from all the other days, except for what took place on it. At about 1.30 or 2 we were about to sit down to a hasty lunch when we heard what we thought was a cheer, we dashed out and saw everyone running in the direction of Lower Mount Street, so we all ran too. We were just in time to see the rebels surrender from Boland's, They had sent an aged lady to the corner with a white flag and she (a civilian non-combatant whose services they secured) negotiated the surrender whereupon about a hundred men, unarmed holding their hands above their heads and displaying a white flag, marched in fours up Grattan Street and lined up in front of Elpis. They were searched and marched off to Ballsbridge. Their leader was a Mexican called De Valera. Being a Mexican I suppose it was his nature to rebel. Bobby was almost under their feet the whole time and secured empty cartridge clips and other valuables which were being thrown away.

Needless to say there was great rejoicing over this, we neglected the snipers who kept quiet for a while and went about freely. Daddy went in a car across town and saw Sackville Street etc., and we knocked off our dressings for the rest of the day. At about 3 o'clock, however, when we were congratulating ourselves all round, an urgent request came from the Castle Hospital that we should do some washing for them, as they were very badly off. Accordingly we started in to wash in our laundry and as all was quiet, we were able to utilize a clothes line which Daddy, Jack and someone else erected in the Square. Alas, that no one had a camera, all went smoothly till about 5.30 when we went to hang out the last lot and found we could not as a sniper had opened fire on the soldiers at the corner.

We hung the rest in the back yard of forty and were about to leave the rest out all night, when the soldiers told Mrs. Heppel Marr (an Englishwoman who was in command of the laundry and who called us "geals") that she must take her washing in, as it obstructed their view across the Square. She and another woman rushed out and got it in safely. This is another testimony of the fact that the Sinn Feiners respected the Red Cross, as that man could have got any one of us, at any time, during the afternoon while we were playing the washing game. This business of course, meant a fresh tattoo all up and down the street, but needless to remark they did not get the sniper, nor, indeed, did he get any of them. The next day Monday was really the last day of the risings. On Saturday and Sunday all the chief places capitulated. Boland's, the G.P.O. (which was shelled), Jacob's, the South Dublin Union, and all the places, in fact, that I mentioned as having been taken in the beginning.

There were, of course, still the snipers and they kept us going on Monday; but after that they just melted away and of course very few of them were caught. We had a grand finale here on Monday morning in the shape of our friend the machine gun on the roof and a sniper in the Grove-White's house in Mount Street Crescent. The Grove-Whites luckily were away. How we missed getting bullets in at the back windows is a mystery. They went everywhere and the din was even worse than it had been on Saturday. During lunch we could hardly hear ourselves speak and we stayed in the back of the house as little as possible. This was the end, however. There has been no more firing since except one incident, of which you shall hear.

Just as we were shutting our work room upstairs having made a fine reserve supply of dressings. Jack came up to ask me if I would care to see Sackville Street. I hurried down and a party of us walked across town, our white uniforms and Red Crosses acting as a passport everywhere. I already tried to describe Sackville Street but I assure you I have failed miserably. The irrepressible Bobby scaled the ruins of the G.P.O. and secured an alarm clock, so bashed you would not know what it was, as a trophy. The whole place was sprinkled with the blue paper tapes on which they take the messages.

I forgot to mention that on Sunday evening Ulick rolled up at dinner time and we heard a lot of news from him. He has come to us every night since, as also Frank Nicholson stationed for the time being at our corner.

We came home through Trinity College and it was a sight worth seeing to see it packed with soldiers and horse lines in all the quads.

In the night we heard sounds of terrific crashes and were afraid the show had started again, but we found that the street lamps had been turned on, and the soldiers being very jumpy and fancying they were exposed by the light, shot the lamps out. Since then the only firing has been guns let off by accident. The Provost says they have no control over their rifles and I don't think he is far wrong.

On Tuesday we took a walk round Stephen's Green. All the houses have their windows smashed and the front of the College of Surgeons is chipped all over with bullet holes. A few of the shops in Grafton Street were looted by the roughs, that apache element which you find in every city and which comes to the surface at times like these. None of the looting was done by the Sinn Feiners, their general behaviour was very good though of course there were exceptions.

On Wednesday we visited Mount Street which I have already described. The Donaldsons' old house at the corner of Haddington Road is a wreck and the place is generally pretty badly bashed about.

I think I have told you the most important parts now though, of course, there is a host of details which we will have to tell you by degrees.

I began this letter on Monday and to-day is Saturday. Yesterday a gas explosion very nearly wrecked O'Connell Bridge but I do not think it is very bad and there does not appear to have been any loss of life.

This morning we had a letter from Uncle Billy and he is to arrive home on leave to-morrow morning! The boys and I are going back on Monday, so we shall see him for one day. I am about 10 days late, they are 3 or 4. It was a mercy in disguise that his and your leave was stopped when it was as it would have been very little of a holiday for either of you to be at home during this row. We were very glad to get your letter (yesterday, as, of course, all the posts were stopped for 10 days) and to hear that you are safe. Uncle Billy seems to think you might get leave at any time now, it will be a pity if we miss you.

It is very sad to think how these rotten Sinn Feiners have let the country down, but, please goodness, they will be dealt with now. Mr. Alton says, they are an extraordinary cross between poets and corner boys, and one cannot help having a deep pity for them, in that they are let astray by their dreams and ideals.

Ulick Daly is off to France; he got 48 hours' notice yesterday and Frank Nicholson is going to Egypt.

There is a nice task before all of us when we go back to England and have to uphold the honour of our country among the Saxons, for we have to make clear to them what is perfectly clear to everyone over here, that this is no Irish Rebellion, but a rising by a minority of the people. And that bad as it is, they were doing a higher thing than going on strike for a rise of wages and that they were ready to die for what they believed.

With much lore from all of us and very best wishes for a pleasant stay at your little village.

Ever your loving sister. Molly.

P.S. You might keep this letter.

Chapter IV

June 1916-1918
"All Men Must Die"

May 22nd, 1916: Thornley to Molly

I am very sorry if my reply to your most interesting narrative has not yet reached you, only I wrote to 39 not knowing what your movements would be.

You show a singular lack of appreciation of my sense of value and tact if you think that anything would make me part from it. I think I will send it home to Mother, it should be typewritten with the rest.

I am glad you are playing cricket, it is a game as I have found that requires and cultivates immense self-control and is really worthwhile playing. Only don't keep an average of the runs you make. I always know if a man is a real cricketer or not, as soon as he tells me his average. Of course all boys don't, but unless you are going to be a pro, and need it as a recommendation it is a useless encumbrance.

The Hun gave us another stewing yesterday - he had a bit of a morning hate, but about 4.30 pip emma - 8.30 he gave us beans with 4th and 6th and 8th and all kinds of gas shells. We were weeping like children in one another's arms by the time he was halfway through. Lachrymatory shells give you a sore throat, sore eyes, a running nose and a splitting headache and is one of the worst horrors of war I have yet experienced. In the middle of the show we had an order to stand by for gas - that is real asphyxiating gas, but I think it was only the H.Q. with cold feet because the wind was never really right for the job all day.

Anyway the Hun is a blighter and needs torture of some kind, the only pity being that at present I can see no chance of his getting it.

We left X---- where we were in rest on the 4th of this month and moved to Y -- where the rest of the brigade was waiting to go out. Here we stayed till the 8th and then moved on to Z--- where we came into action in place of D battery 62nd who went into rest with the rest (A JOAK)[42]. Here we have been kept rather lively by one or two visitations of Hun wrath such as I described overleaf.

My finger on which I think I told you I had an abscess was extremely painful for a time but is now in fact it has nothing to do but heal up now.

No more news so will dry up now.

Your loving Thornley.

---

[42] Rowan's expression – see Chapter II.

June 6th, 1916: Lady Woods to Molly

My dearest Molly,

Your letter, and one from Thornley, with the same news in both, arrived last night. This is to tell you that you must get home not later than Sat. morning, as there is a rumour that all ingress is to be stopped for Whitsuntide. They don't give it to you. They are evidently preparing for an outbreak on Sunday or Monday, and if you wait you may not be able to get here for a fortnight.

"They" means the military, not the Sinn Feiners — I hardly think even the latter could be mad enough to risk another Rising; though Mr. Millar, of the College of Surgeons, was stopped at Leeson St. Bridge last night, and told not to go on, as they were sniping — the sentries are back on all the bridges now. They were off for about ten days. We have never really been free from sniping, though we all go about as usual, but sometimes there are shots quite near. There are about ten times as many rebels now as there were before the Rebellion, and Mr. Millar told your Father that everyone in the street is wearing Sinn Fein buttons and colours openly. I haven't noticed it myself. Green, white and yellow.

Better wait for a telegram from me on Thursday, as there is no use chucking your term unless Thor is really home.[43]

I don't think you need worry your old head about the naval battle. If the Germans, who shrieked "Victory" at first, are screaming for "Vengeance" now, I think we can afford to smile indulgently. As for the ships and the men, of course we must lose both to win the War, and though there is more at a blow there is nothing like the wastage going on at Sea as there is by Land. And think of our gallant Beatty attacking 40 of them with 8 ships! I nearly cried with pride over it. Anyway we downed more Huns than they did Britons. The thing that cut me to the heart was that when they thought we had had a bad knock there were bonfires and rejoicing all round Rathfarnham way. We are a rotten nation, and I don't think there is the smallest hope for us. The decent people are bound to go under in this new settlement. It is simply being made in terror of the Sinn Fein movement — a rotten reason for doing anything. There is only one way of governing Ireland, and that is by a Military Dictator — Sir John Maxwell would do nicely for the present.

Well goodbye for the present, my dear, I shall be glad to see my two eldest home again.

Love from Daddy and heaps from your loving Mother.

---

[43] Students at Cambridge had to "keep term." If Molly came home early she would lose a term and have to make it up during the summer.

June 23rd, 1916: Thornley to Molly

My dear Molly

I am very sorry for not writing to you before but we have been very busy lately, and I'm afraid just a bit lazy too. This is the pen that we gave to Pembry that day that we went shopping. Life out here is very quiet as regards the Hun wo has let us alone for the present and is evidently engaging his overdeveloped brain in further schemes for our destruction. We quite expect to see him roll up a 50 ton shell or a railway loco full of high explosive (set running on a prepared track at 70 m.p.h. towards our lines) or something of that violent nature but still we contain our souls impatience and sit tight. I think that the long looked-for peace will still be a bit long in coming but of course one can never tell.

There is rather a good tale about the Australians I heard from a man on the boat coming back here. The said gentleman arrived in the trenches with a certain amount of eclat and the triumphal progress was only marred by the appearance the next morning of a hoarding about 10 feet by 20 over the Hun line.

Advance Australia! (if you can)

These blighters know all the small things and so I think the large ones are not hid from them. Still as we know as much about them the balance is pretty equal.

No more news. Loads of love to all, Your loving brother Thornley.

June 24th 1916: Billy to Molly
D Battery, 102nd Brigade, R.F.A

My dear Molly,

I'm afraid I have neglected you in the way of letters lately but there are great doings afoot and consequently life has been strenuous and leisure scarce. We were pulled out of the line about a week ago and taken into reserve and today we move again to an entirely different part of La Belle France. The place we are going to may possibly remind you of the station from which you would start to go and play golf at the Island. After that all is mystery but rumour is rife. I was awfully glad to hear that Thornley had been home on leave and that he was looking fit. I had a letter from him not long ago in which he told me that there was a possibility of his getting away but things are so uncertain nowadays that I wasn't sure if he'd bring it off. I think it was most reprehensible of you chucking your term at Cambridge just to see your little brother but what chiefly worries me is what the fire brigade is going to do.

Any day I expect to hear that Cambridge has been razed (no, that's a misprint) burned to the ground by a devastating fire and what will your feelings be in after years when you reflect that had you not let your fraternal feelings overcome your thirst for knowledge you would have been there to hose the reel or unreel the hose, which sounds rather indelicate, or whatever it is you do and have squelched the fire in its incipiency. However I trust that my fears will prove groundless. I shudder to think of the expense you are laying up for me in the near future by undoing all the trouble I took in training the pup to efface himself instantly and effectively on the approach of the ticket collector. He had reached as nearly as possible the acme of perfection when war broke out and now to think that you bloated plutocrats are negativing all my efforts. I don't know when I will be able to post this letter, as we are moving in about half an hour. Tell your Mother that her cakes all arrived safely but you might also remind her that she hasn't written to me once since I came back from home. Love to all at Rathleigh. Ever your loving uncle, Billy

DD: *Billy Shaw was serving in the 102th Brigade of the Royal Field Artillery, which saw action in the battle of the Loos, 25 September - 14 October 1915, the Somme in 1916, the battle of Messines 7-14 June 1917 and the Battle of Passchendaele which began on 31 July 1917. He was awarded the Distinguished Service Order for his actions in Mametz Wood at this time. The citation, dated January 19th, 1917 reads:*

> *"On the 28th of July near Mametz position of Division 102 was being shelled – Major Shaw who was a little distance away immediately ran up to the position and found that a dump of S.A.A. and bombs nearby had been set on fire; he obtained some water and although heavy shelling continued personally extinguished the fire. After seeing to the removal of some wounded men of his battery Major Shaw saw that another fire had occurred close to No. 1 gun pit, this he also personally extinguished being under shell fire the whole time."*
>
> *Lieut-Colonel H. Wilkinson*
AA and QMG 23rd Division

July 30th 1916: Thornley to Molly
France

My dearest Molly

Thank you very much indeed for all your nice parcels. I have received 2 cakes, 1 tongue and potted meat, and one writing pad since I wrote to you last. As you may very well imagine I have not had extra much time to write home to you but I have been sending F.P.C.'s as often as I could get hold of them.

I am writing this at 7.30 a.m. in what was once No Man's Land where we have been working like slaves for some time I have had the most appalling time since I wrote last time and have been converted into one of those despicable "peace at any price" merchants in every sense. Of course, I cannot tell you any more except that the papers are generally overoptimistic and that the war will last till the end of summer 1917, unless that is to say someone of the many reasons that the Hun will collapse are true, which I can hardly believe. We are of course not happy or comfortable but our spirits are, if anything, better. "The spirit of our troops is excellent" and we are managing very creditably in consequence.

The Hun of course is not playing the game. He is a spiteful beggar and does his worst to annoy us at every possible moment. He thinks absolutely nothing of shelling us violently during dinner (absolutely tabooed by the Hague Convention) or spoiling our beauty sleep with lachrymatory shells or some other noxious form of stimulant (definitely banned by the Cologne Conference). All this is annoying and curiously enough instead of steeling my heart and nerving my arm for further effort, the only effect it leaves on me is to make me heartily wish that the war was over and yours truly was back in dear old Blighty.

This is all guff, so in view of the paper famine I will confine it to one page.

Your loving Thornley

August 4th, 1916: Thornley to Molly
France

Dearest Molly,

Thank you very much indeed for your two letters, both of which sound desperately busy and excited. I was glad to hear Patricia was doing so well and Mother too.

We have been having the deuce of a time here lately and opportunities for sleep have been conspicuous by their absence but we are all very cheery all the time and working like blacks both mentally and physically. I am on top hole form and am fed up with this here offensive to the back teeth.

The weather out here is simply roasting, and walking along or even sitting in a trench where one cannot get any air is the most trying thing I know.

Naturally I cannot tell you how we are getting on, but with luck the war should be over by this autumn. I personally think that we shall have to carry on without luck.

With love and best wishes to all your loving brother, Thornley

August 12th, 1916   Thornley to Molly
France

My dearest Molly

Many happy returns of yesterday. I had omitted entirely to write to you because I was up to the ears in work and was very slack and weary. We have had the hell of a time out here for the last fortnight and after building 3 battery positions in the last 10 days are reasonably comfortable in the second one we built. The third of which 1 told you was never occupied, we were spared that, but we had it nearly finished all the same.

Jack tells me that you are having it hot in Recess.[44] Let me remind him that out here the average temp. for the last 14 days was 77 degrees in the ammunition racks which is the coolest place in the battery and through all that we have had to dig and work and sweat up to the trenches carrying tons of equipment. 1 am worn to a shadow, i.e. 1 have lost about 12 stone dead in the time and am consequently able to take cover with remarkable speed and in the most unlikely places.

There is very little news, the war is still on and looks as if it was going to fizzle out in due course. (N.B. This is a perfectly safe statement and entitles the speaker to say "I told you so" no matter what the events my prove to be). We are all hoping for a rest but don't look like getting one for years and years to come.

Give my love to all at home and tell them to K.T. the Recess Hotel F.B. till I roll along myself and show them how to land a salmon in Inagh.[45] Best wishes for the fishing but tell them that if it does rain in Galway it won't rain in France.

Your loving bro, Thornley

P.S. Thanks so much for the parcel. Chicken was absolutely top hole and may be repeated as often as you like. The sausages were a bit off when they arrived and I think the weather is a bit unsuitable still. Thanks all the same. Thank Jack for his letter and tell him that doubtless I will write to him before many months are past.

August 12th, 1916: Billy to Molly
D Battery, France

My dear Molly,

Many thanks for your letters which are very welcome. Though my feelings when I read about your being at Recess were rather like what Tantalus's must have been when he saw the mug of beer and him with a thirst on him that would float the big Lizzie. Heartiest congratulations on your bronze medal of. St. John of Jerusalem, but don't forget that all the best people call him Sinjun.

Our relief takes place on Monday next by which time we will have been in the battle practically six weeks, so it isn't coming any too soon. I had a great show the other day, I was up in the front trenches observing when I saw a Bosch bombing party coming down a sap to attack a party of ours who were working up to it. My telephone wire was intact at the moment and I was able to turn my battery on, we gave them a quick dose and when the smoke and dust cleared away, the Bosch of where was he? Your knowledge of the English classics and especially of that beautiful poem "Casablanca" will enable you to finish the story. We are still going

---

[44] The family were holidaying in the village of Recess in Connemara.
[45] Lough Inagh is renowned for its fishing

strong out here and progressing slowly but surely. I think that the end must be very nearly in sight, what between us, the French, the Russkis and the Italians the old Bosch must be having a very poor time.

It will be great if we get that there houseboat. By Gad how I am looking forward to my dolce fa viente on the after deck abaft the galley with a pot of beer in one hand and a pipeful of Mitchell's exotica mild in the other while the good ship is propelled by the joint efforts of the Woods family and the pup down the sylvan glades under Leeson Street Bridge. Then indeed will I find peace with all the world even the wily Hun. I suppose you are having a splendid time in Recess. I'm sorry the dry weather is spoiling Robert's fishing. We could do with a drop of rain out here ourselves. The heat is terrific, the dust appalling, the flies overwhelming and the smell, phew!!! Words fail me. A dead Bosch is very nearly as unpleasant as a live one but anyhow they're in no tra-a-nce. By the way I completely forgot to tell you that I had been wounded but it was such a little one that I hadn't the face to report it. It was a very tiny piece of shell in the arm and I was inordinately proud of it for four days till I woke up on the fifth and found to my intense disgust that it had disappeared. Sic transit gloria mundi, from which you will see that my French is improving!

By the way when you get back to Dublin there is a corporal of mine in the Castle Hospital suffering from gas poisoning (we all get a touch of that, but he was rather bad). His name is Cpl. Hart, R.F.A. and if you have nothing better to do you might drop in and see him and take him a few Woodbines. If you tell him you are my niece he will receive you with open arms. I'm afraid there is no prospect of any leave yet a bit but it will be all the better when it does come. Love to all the family and the pup.

Ever your affectionate Uncle Billy.

August 18th, 1916 Thornley to Molly
France

My dearest Molly,

Thank you very much for the parcels which you and Mother sent me. I got one four days ago from Findlater's with tongue, cake and potted meat in it, all very acceptable and in good condition.

I hope and think that we have finished with the push for the moment (a fortnight, I hope), but one can never tell. N.B. this is strictly confidential.

Thanks very much for your letters, you were always an A.1. Correspondent. I had a letter from Daddy written from the boat on Inagh and he seems to be having a simply top hole time. I only wish I could join you all there. This war seems to me to be a most appalling waste of time, here am I with all my education to finish, wasting away in an obscure farm without the consolation of having helped on the push beyond the extent of the ordinary work of a subaltern, and with no prospect of dong any useful work for a long time to come, at the same time I do not think I could conjugate duco now if it was to save my life.

Our poor infantry have been wiped out twice, once on the 3rd of July when the battalions numbered on an average about 200 strong and once between the 28th July and the 13th August when the same thing recurred. This is really why we are resting the Div. Artillery has not suffered at all lately really.

Well when the war's over and we all get together again there are two things you must remember in your arrangements for subsequent holiday making. (1) I must not be asked to camp out in any circumstances and (2) sandbags and digging are absolutely taboo, so if Bobby has any bright schemes in his head for pitching a tent in the back garden or building a deep dugout on Loughlinstown

Common or any other fine place he may "take a large hoe and a shovel also and dig till he gently perspires" and if he asks me so much as to look on I'll take him by the seat of his pants and show him what the mine did to the Hun when it went off.

There is a great story going round here of an incident that occurred to a Tommy of Lloyd's old regiment the Buffs, and was told me by an officer of that ilk that I met in the trenches. The regt had attacked and taken a trench in the early part of the push when a Hun about 7ft 2 inches high rushed out of a German dugout and seized hold of the aforesaid Tommy (who stood about 3ft 6in with his boots on) by the scruff of his neck and the slack of his pants and carried him screaming and kicking, biting and stabbing at some length to the British lines. The Buffs themselves did not shoot as they were afraid of hurting Tommy. Arrived at the safest spot he could find he jumped down into the trench, deposited the almost purple Thomas on the fire step to recover and cool off and said "Ver goot - you haf me captured!" Your loving brother, Thornley.

Aug 22nd, 1916: Thornley to Molly
France

My dearest Molly,
Thank you very much indeed for your two letters of the 18th and the 13th, the former I received today. You seem to have been fishing pretty hard and it seems a great pity that you have not been rewarded even by a compliment, still if you stick to it I dare say you may move Festi of Stephen to a display of that politeness which I am sure is innate in their souls. Thanks very much for the notes and map which you returned. I never used them and do not want them so there is no harm done. Still I must be more careful next time, that is the worst of mixing private affairs with business, you never know where it will land you.

Thanks also for envelopes enclosed, they will come in very useful. I am not using one on this letter as I have succeeded in sponging on someone else for paper and envelopes.

The weather out here has improved after the rather wet spell we had and although it is not nearly so hot as it was before it is quite fine. Of course one is not allowed to say anything but these cheerful fellows round here are making all arrangements for 2 more years campaign. I do not of course mean the authorities but the denizens military of this part of the line. They are a lazy lot of blighters as far as I can see and took very little trouble with their work.

There is very little news, things are dragging along and the 3rd year of the war looks as if it would be just like the other two as far at any rate as we are concerned. Your loving bro, Thornley

August 30th 1916: Thornley to Molly
France

My dear Molly,

I thank you very much for your letter. So you have felt the delicious sensation of a tug on your line and played your first fish. I suppose my nature is a bit crude and I always hanker for so big a fish that the sensations will be very definite, but for you whose nature is more finely strung a 1lb fish of fighting propensities should be ample.

We are having a very easy and very happy time here, except for the fact that it rains all day and every day and houses below the ground are apt to fill very quickly and being full of water they have not even the resort of remaining full. My note on the matter of the summer after the war goes emphatically for Quaple Lodge (?). I do not of course wish to disparage the House Boat which I think would be simply At1 but the more solid comfort of a real house is much more attractive to me than anything connected with water, at the present moment. We must organise croquet on the back lawn when this is over, the beauty of it being that Billy and I by the virtue of our training will lick the rest of you into socks. I will then show you what indirect laying on a target you cannot see can do. You might however have the croquet balls fitted with dial sights.

Much love and best wishes, your loving brother, Thornley

September 9th, 1916: Thornley to Molly
France

Thank you very much indeed for your letter. I have just finished writing to Jack and finding that yours was the only letter not answered I decided that it was worthwhile to polish you off as well. This may not sound very complimentary but it is true, and if Jack lets you read his letter you will realise that truth is a luxury and will not grudge me the rudeness.

I am glad to see that your attitude in life has become more healthy and that you have at last fallen in love even if it is with a Count of 70 summers, (some count) (A JOAK HA!HA!) You may be quite sure that he was secretly enamoured of you. But that his innate nobleness of character compelled him to shrink from offering you a match which would only have laid you open to the accusation of having married for money.

What is a News peg? You say you have bought some news pegs to play croquet with and I don't quite understand; is it a kind of daily bulletin or an official communique? News is what we all want but why have it on, in, by, with or from pegs? I suppose the clips are to keep the pegs of news in when you get them [This joak has gone far enough, Ed.][46]

I hope you are carrying out my scheme of indirect croquet playing where you can never see the ball you are aiming at. The dial sights required are called Sights dial No.7 Mark I. Only if you wanted four you would have to say Sights dial Mark I four, and state your reason for writing.

Ever since we came to this position I have been so busy stating my reasons in writing that it is quite a pleasant change to state something in writing that is not reasonable.

Leave is beginning again for officers who have extra special cases, and they of course have to state their reasons in writing too. I have to put in under four different names, and put in four separate reasons for each name but I am afraid I will not get it as it is almost impossible to trace the three fictitious names as members of AJ62 and the Adjutant may smell a rat. (To put it vulgarly, I am sure he smells plenty every night if he lives in the kind of dug-out that I am in, but that is not the kind I mean).

There is a great advantage about the New Army and that is that whatever you want done can be done by a man whose job it has been before the war. Thus I have got a gamekeeper and a poacher hard at work snaring partridges for the mess in a little coppice nearby. The competition is tremendous and I believe the bets in the battery are up to 100 francs all told. So far nothing has happened and I am beginning to fear that they have joined forces and that the whole battery are feasting on partridges some of which at any rate should have found their way to the officers' mess. If nothing has happened by tomorrow I shall remove the bullet from a revolver cartridge and do the Heath Robinson's "freelance" touch with some old nails and things (mostly things, I expect) and see if I can't do something that way.

It is really too late to write any more so I will stop.

Your loving brother, Thornley

September 11th 1916: Thornley to Molly
France

Thanks so much for your letter received this afternoon. So Bobby has been tight already, the little beast! I expect he even has the audacity to deny it. Ask him from if he had a "mouth" and a "head" in the morning. I suppose the fact of his getting his hair cut the next day points to:

1. A desire for coolth in that overheated member

---

[46] "Ed." In this case is Lady Margaret Woods.

2. A resolution to turn over a new leaf and a symbolic signification of the fact (you will remember that St. Paul "shaved his head at Caesarea, for he had a vow").

I have just returned from the O.P. where I have had 48 hours duty. It is curious how childish the infantry are over the artillery. Any officer off duty comes up to me in the O.P. when I am up there and as it is only 25 yards behind the front line we get a good view. The company commander was up there this morning while I was shooting at a hostile machine gun emplacement. He was simply overjoyed because I hit the thing and nearly knocked me off the perch I was sitting on the way he jumped about with excitement. He then dashed out and told the infantry colonel what a jolly fine lot of gunners we were and generally cracked us up, all over a not very creditable performance of what is supposed to be our job carried out under ideal conditions. Some indeed "have greatness thrust upon them."

You say you have been playing Nap, we find that vingt-et-un is a more relaxing game for the mind - not to mention the morals - and it is played in most companies in the line. As we join a mess for the time it is in there and eat with them we also play cards with them and get very chummy generally. So that O.P. under the present ideal conditions of good company, good food and execrable drink is really a very pleasant job, especially as the Hun is quite quiet and there is plenty of water for washing. That is why we have taken to spending 48 instead of 24 hours up there.

I am afraid I am talking shop a dreadful deal so will continue by wishing you all the best of luck. Tell Bobby to be careful with his nose pointing, it's been the death of many.

Your loving brother, Thornley

September 20th 1916: Thornley to Molly
France

My dear Molly,

You seem to be having the deuce of a time with your "peculiar type of madman" however the type from what I can gather from your rather distracted letter does not seem to be dangerous.

I suppose in the midst of your various excitements such a drab thing as war will hardly interest you, nevertheless as I have nothing else to talk about I must take the risk of boring you. We are at present billeted in a village and the people are living here just as usual apparently oblivious to the fact that the Huns are a short mile away. Periodically my landlady comes in and strafes the servants for making a mess in the kitchen, she is very voluble about it and they get rather tired of saying "no compret" to her. Yesterday I heard the tornado burst with more than usual vehemence and last for more than the usual length of time, in a lull between her squalls a quiet voice remarked "No wonder these 'ere French people gets old quick, Bill, it must be a dreadful strain on you talking that langwidge."

Leave has reopened and I think: that with any luck I should get home in time for the Christmas holidays. I shall try to do so in any case it would be great fun seeing you all again.

We have been having great fun with the detached section, it is a chance of showing one's efficiency and I am beginning to be quite energetic about it, which is a new and really quite pleasing experience. We have been finding targets everywhere and shooting at everything within sight - as the only targets allowed are machine guns and trench mortar batteries, the number of these has increased like anything. In fact it is a question of supply and demand, and they simply have to be there if we want to shoot at any particular point.

Life has settled down into a routine again although a very interesting one at that so news is not very plentiful. I will therefore close with expressions of esteem and regard which I can only hope are entirely reciprocated (Humph)

Your loving brother

Brief message from Meg to Molly

My darling,
Thornley was killed on Oct. 27. There isn't anything to say to you – but we must be brave.

With all my love,
Your loving Mother

November 9th, 1916: Billy to Molly
Head Quarters 102nd Bde R.F.A

My dearest Molly,
Your note came as a great shock to me, it was the first intimation I had had and then I saw the confirmation in Monday's paper. I can't tell you how I feel for you, having lost a brother myself I know and realize something of what you're going through now. Your pluck in sticking it out alone in Cambridge touched me very deeply. It is awfully hard to say anything in consolation that doesn't sound hackneyed and banal but I think a feeling of pride in your brother's supreme self-sacrifice for all that decent men hold sacred will supersede over your grief in time. He has given his life for his country. No man can do more and you would not have had your brother do less. I am feeling awfully anxious about your mother, but I also feel sure that her pride and splendid courage will come to her aid.

Will you let me know as soon as possible how she is?

It is awful out here at present, letters and papers sometimes taking as much as a fortnight to reach us.

God bless you, my dear old girl,
Ever your loving uncle, Billy

November 1st, 1916: Meg to Molly
39 Merrion Square

My darling Child,

We have a small grain of comfort to-day. He was asleep in his dugout when the shell fell and death must have been instantaneous. In fact, he probably never knew anything – simply never wakened. The telegram said "died of wounds." I did not tell you as I wanted to spare you what I have suffered for 24 hours, with visions of horror and pain – but now we know it was swift and merciful. I have no comfort to offer you but that, but my dear I know what he was to you and what your loss and sorrow is and you have my heart's whole sympathy. Your father thinks you ought not to come home, but we don't want to be Spartan about it. He thinks we shall fight out these dreadful days better alone, and that your work and being with strangers will help you, but if you feel you must come, my darling, just do. It is much to have you left and the other three. We had a letter from him this morning written on Oct. 26th – the day before – and he was well.

Would you like to wear black? It is entirely a matter for yourself – you know how little it matters, but if it would feel better to do it let me know what you want sent.

Darling, time is the only softener of a blow like this. We must just set our teeth and endure – there is no comfort and no short cut. In time, the pain will lessen and the pride in his glorious manhood dominates us, but we have a hard road to travel.

With all my love, dearest,
Ever your loving Mother.

November 3rd, 1916: Robert to Molly
39 Merrion Square

My dearest Molly,

The more I think of it the better it seems that we are all separated so that we can get over the first acuteness of our grief without the aggravation of seeing one another in it. We must first bear up and remember that it can't and never could be helped, for it was impossible for him to have done anything except what he thought he ought to do.

Mother is keeping wonderfully well like the Trojan she is. Everyone has been most kind and sympathetic and doing their best to mitigate the severity of the blow. We have not yet heard from Billy, I suppose his first intimation will have been from Mother.

The boys are well,
Your loving father, R.H. Woods

November 13th, 1916: H Hughes to Cyril Sutherin

My dear Sutherin,

I am afraid I can tell you very little about that awful night. It seems like a nightmare to me even and I can hardly imagine what it must have been like for you. You were right about poor Woods. It is too awfully sad and we have all felt it most fearfully. He was just breathing when we got him out but by the time we reached the Dressing Station he was dead. I was asleep when the shell burst that did the damage. I heard a crash and got up and went outside. All was quiet and I hadn't the least idea where the shell had gone. I rang up the telephonist and asked if any of the shells had fallen in the Batty.

They said that most were in front but that one had fallen near their dug out but they didn't think any damage was done. I thought everything all right and went back to bed. This was about 10 p.m. At about 12.15 a.m. Cpl. Rainsford woke me up and said your dug out was blown in and he could hear you outside. I got hold of about six men and 2 stretcher- bearers and we got both of you out in about 10 min. I went with you to the Dr. Stat. and you fell off the stretcher once, the Doc said you would be all right. We spent some time with poor old Woods but it was too late.

That is all there is to tell but it is awful to think what you two must have suffered. However it does no good thinking about it, etc., etc. H. Hughes

November 20th, 1916: Cyril Sutherin to Jack
C/o J. Rushbrooke, Esq., J.P. Bulmershe Court,
Earley, Bucks

Dear Woods,

I am writing you this letter as I thought perhaps you would like some further details concerning your brother's death at the front. Which I can give you as I was with him at the time.

Of course it is quite impossible for me to tell you how very very sorry I am for you all and I would have liked to have written to your Sister or Mother but since they must still be suffering from terrible shock which the news of his death must have caused them I thought I would write to you and then you could show them this letter or not at your discretion.

Although you doubtless do not know my name, I had been closely associated with poor Thornley since April last and we always shared a dug out and were together on that terrible night when your brother died.

The Batty position was some 200 yds S. of FLERS village and the conditions were very bad in every sense.

Thornley and I had constructed a little dugout in a shallow hole with sandbagged sides and some curved iron for roof and it served very well as shelter from the wet, though it was in no way shellproof, none of us having any protection from shell fire.

At about 9.30 p.m., just after we had gone to bed (in our clothes) the enemy started to shell us. We thought it useless moving from our shelter as it was a pitch black night and everywhere deep shell holes full of liquid mud and no one spot safer than another.

Within a few minutes a big shell fell close beside us and blew in the whole dugout completely, burying poor old Thornley and myself.

We were stunned for a short while and then found that although we could just talk to each other we could neither of us move an inch in any part of our body.

At first we were able to breathe fairly well, but as time elapsed it became increasingly difficult and the pressure on our bodies from the weight of earth and on our lungs through the lack of air was terrible and our limbs gradually became cramped and numbed. By this time we fully realised that nothing short of a miracle could save us and we had only sufficient breath to talk to each other and could not shout.

Your brother, like the brave boy he was, died knowing it must be the end, yet with his thoughts only for you all at home and for the safety of his men.

It is quite impossible for me to express my feelings in writing, but I wanted to write and tell you how brave Thornley was right up to the last.

As you will see by the enclosed copy of letter I received from another officer in the Battery, the help we prayed for came eventually but just too late to save your brother – a few more minutes and it would have been too late also for me.

As regards myself I am fortunate enough to have left hospital on sick leave and expect to be quite fit very shortly.

Will you please convey to your family my deepest sympathy. I have lost a true friend in Thornley who has died for his Country like so many brave Irishmen.

Sincerely yours, Cyril Sutherin.

November, 24th 1916: Billy to Molly
102nd Brigade, R.F.A

My dear Molly,

I was awfully glad to get your letters dated 17th and 19th and very much relieved to have such a good account of both your Father and Mother. I have had letters from them both and they are evidently displaying great courage.

It is the parents who have to bear all the hardships of this war. I think you were quite right to go home for a week. They both said what a comfort it had been to them. What I meant in my first letter was that I was impressed by your not telling anyone at Cambridge about it but stuck it out alone. I don't see any prospect of getting home on leave until the region of the New Year, but I am looking forward more than I can say to seeing you all then. I had a letter from poor little Patsy, I'm afraid she's a bit down on her luck, but she's so young she will soon buck up.

Thanks you so much for your congratulations on my D.S.O. The D.S.O. comes immediately after my name until I get a V.C. (Open the window! How ???). Then R.F.A. follows after. I hope you met and talked with the great Miss Clough. I never heard of her myself but doubtless that though not my fault is my misfortune. Your scheme of chucking work and taking to novels is an excellent one provided you take to the right novels. I believe your education will thereby be greatly enhanced. I am writing this under the stress of much work with little time to do it in, so by for the Concerto, as we say in Esperanto.

Ever your loving uncle, Billy

December 18th 1916: William Shaw to Robert Woods

My dear Robert,

I have not written to you before because I was waiting for a reply to my letter to Thornley's C.O. I have now had it. He was asleep with another officer in his dugout when a shell crashed through and there is no doubt that death was absolutely instantaneous in fact it seems to be very doubtful if he had time to wake up at all.

This news was a great relief to me and I am sure will prove a slight consolation to you at all events. I have also got the exact location of his grave which of course is enclosed in the usual way and will be kept decently by a corps out here for that purpose solely called the Graves Registration Committee. Thornley must have been in a couple of miles of me when he was killed but of course out here it is almost impossible to find out where everybody is. Had I known soon enough I would have gone over and seen his grave but we are now over 100 miles from there. I hope to be coming home on leave sometime in Jan. and am looking forward more than I can say to seeing you all again. I think that in spite of Roumania things are looking very healthy, this peace-kite of the Kaiser's is an obvious confession of weakness, the only anxiety about it out here is whether it will be rejected with the contumely it deserves. I auger great things from D.L-G. I don't think now the end can be delayed beyond next winter, we're going to give 'em fair hell in the spring. Love to all at 39 and all best wishes of the season.

Your affec. brother-in-law, Wm. Shaw

December 19th 1916: Billy to Molly
France

My dear Molly,

Thanks very much for your letters. We have now finished our march and are waiting to go up into action again. We had quite a good time as we marched practically through the whole of Northern France. I enjoyed it very much and the weather on the whole was wonderful, cold but dry.

It's very bad luck on you having to "keep term" but I gather from your letters that it was not very strenuous. The illogicality of the proceeding is obvious but you will find as you grow older that there is a sad lack of logic in the meaning of most things in the world. I don't think there is any occasion to be pessimistic about the War news at present, however bad things like Greece and Roumania may appear superficially, there can be no doubt that the Hun has no illusions left now as to who will be the ultimate victor and the rejection of his peace proposals will not make it any easier for him as far as his soldiers are concerned. They are, I believe convinced that peace is in sight, and when they have to buckle to and start to fight again they will be worse off than if it had never been mooted. It's like stopping a heavily laden horse on the middle of a steep hill, he has to overcome his inertia before he starts again. Leave is at last definitely in sight and I hope to get home fairly early in January when you will all be at home. I am looking forward to it more than I can say. I am enclosing a trifle as a cadeau de Noel and also as a mark of my affection and esteem for your character and attainments, which have never been displayed to greater advantage than in the last two months.

With all best wishes for Xmas and the New Year. Ever my dear Molly. Your loving uncle, Billy.

February 16th, 1917: Billy to Molly
102nd Bde.R.F.A.

My dear Molly,
Many thanks for all your letters. I was so glad to hear that the melodrama went off satisfactorily and I hope that the competition will be equally so. I had a letter from your Father the other day and the only thing that seemed to worry him about the election was the manhandling that his embryo professional brethren gave him in their enthusiasm for his candidature. His chassis I am glad to say is the only part of him that's feeling sore. I hope to be home on leave early in March, I suppose there is no chance of your being at home then. I expect to reach Ireland for about ten days on March 1st or 2nd but of course can't say for certain. I am looking forward to a holiday enormously.

Ever your loving Uncle, Billy.

DD: *Meanwhile Billy, now Major William Maxwell Shaw, received a mention in despatches dated November 15, 1916:*

"He went forward to ascertain the exact situation of our advanced infantry. Later with another officer and two bombers he carried out a daring reconnaissance of a trench thought to be occupied by the enemy, thereby obtaining most valuable information."
                Winston S. Churchill, Sec. of State for War

May 21st, 1917: Molly to Billy
Clough Hall, Newnham College, Cambridge

My dear Uncle Billy,
There is a custom here called "sleeping on the roof" in which I indulged for two nights last week. To be strictly accurate what I did was waking on the roof. We are not allowed to take out any college property for these diversions which

means improvising your bed out of rugs and cushions and coats. Some people enjoy it, I did not.

I bathed twice in our unutterable Cam but then the weather got cold and I have not been in since.

I rode out beyond the Gog Magog hills on Thursday. Hills is a courtesy title. They are hillocks but you get a fine view over the surrounding plain from them. There is a Roman road along the top of them which is very fine but in a bad state of preservation. There is no sign of pavement but it is as straight as an arrow.

I think Mother and Daddy are coming over at the end of this term to stay with the Master. I am looking forward immensely to showing them Newnham, which Daddy has not seen from the inside. They will see it under more favourable conditions than you did as of course the summer makes a difference in everything.

We have had a lot of rain in the last week but the weather is warm again.

There is no more news except that the Triposes have begun. Everybody is working very hard and is either in a frightful panic or very calm, unnaturally so. I am glad mine does not come off for another year.

DD: *This letter was returned with the words "Killed in Action" written on the envelope.*

James Rowan Shaw
Pont du Hem Military Cemetery, La Gorgue

William Maxwell Shaw
Railway Dugouts Burial Ground, Ypres, Belgium

W Thornley Stoker Woods
Guards Cemetery, Lesboeufs

DD: *In April, 2010, I went with my son Gilbert and grandson William on a tour of the Somme, visiting the three graves pictured here as well as the Thiepval Memorial, the Ulster Tower, the Lochnagar Crater and the preserved trenches at Beaumont Hamel. This brought history alive to us all.*

Poem written by Thornley

"All Men Must Die"

All men must die, but woe the day
    When death his dreadful toll demands
We are all bound to own his sway
    To feel his hands.

All men must die, so why lament?
    Who knows what lies beyond the grave?
If any power on mercy bent
    Thy sins will lave?

And if 'tis grief beyond our life
    Inevitable 'tis to die,
And if 'tis joy, the end of strife
    Is sweet goodbye

For soon we meet, though soon we part
    And oh how sweet that meeting be
When past is all our sins' dull smart
    How happy we!

So when our day is past and we
    Feel life's red setting sun is nigh
Think, that in ending we are free
    And men must die

Chapter V

Gilbert in Trinity College
Letters from his family 1914-1918

Introduction

On his return from Germany, Gilbert Waterhouse was appointed Professor of German at Trinity College, Dublin. Having been in the Officers' Training Corps in England, he found himself one of the few O.T.C. members still in the College during the Easter vacation of 1916 when the Rising began. This chapter contains his first-hand account of the defence, under his command, of the College and the surrounding area during the following days. He was rewarded by the gratitude of the traders of Grafton Street which the quick actions of the O.T.C. had saved from destruction.

This Chapter is taken up with Gilbert Waterhouse's family, mostly through letters written to him by his father and mother. Letters from his brother Hugh who was fighting in France have not survived, but there are many local references to his exploits, with comments clarifying them, written by Gilbert. Included also are a

number of letters written to Mrs. Waterhouse by Arthur and George, two young cousins of hers who were fighting with the Anzac forces in France. Their grandfather, Daniel Wadsworth, had emigrated to Otago, New Zealand c. 1861, and reared a large family.

Harold Waterhouse's family, and that of his wife Sarah Helen Jackson, were close neighbours in the Heywood area of Lancashire, and in 1915, Harold was coming up to his retirement from the Yorkshire and Lancashire Railway, which he had joined about 1876 at the age of eighteen. My father says of him that "he had a very clear brain and great organizing ability. He began as a junior clerk. If he could have started higher up and made contact with the higher executives sooner he would have had all the ability to become general manager. He was a wonderful mixer, had the art of talking on equal terms with platelayers and top brass, never hurt any man's feelings, and had the highest sense of duty to his employers but suffered in his career through not being sufficiently aggressive. He was essentially a quiet man and waited for promotion instead of energetically looking for it."

Sarah Helen's father, John Jackson, was the tenant of Hope Carr Farm, Leigh, for 49 years. He moved to the Rowe Farm, Risley, about 1896, but his son, John Joseph, continued the tenancy for two or three years, living alone there. At the urgent request of his mother John gave up Hope Carr and went to help his parents at the Rowe. Gilbert remembered staying at Hope Carr about 1894-6. Two little cousins, John and William, sons of his uncle George Jackson, played with him there. Uncle George died of pneumonia c.1894 and the children died of diphtheria in 1895.

I remember my grandmother well when she came after Harold's death to live with us in Belfast. My sisters and I loved her company, and her sometimes mischievous sense of humour. She was a great walker and enjoyed going to one of the cinemas in the Lisburn Road, the "Regal" or the "Majestic," often enjoying a swing with us in the little park at Cranmore in her buttoned boots, chuckling at the "six stone" weight limit on the swings which she claimed she did not exceed. She was talented as well, brought her own piano with her, and wrote poems which my father had published under the penname "Hilda"[47]. Her younger sister Jenny we also loved. She had married a wealthy man and when widowed, settled again in Lancashire with the other sister Elizabeth (Lizzy), mentioned in these letters, who aspired to be a novelist but was left unmarried to care for her aging father in the old farm.

Letters from Gilbert Waterhouse's Parents from Heywood, Lancs 1915 – 1918 with notes by G.W.

October 26th, 1915: Father to Gilbert

Dear Gilbert

I enclose Hughie's last letter dated Oct. 20th which arrived here on Sunday. They appear to be all right in the messing department but the condition of affairs that compels him to keep his boots on for 7 days speaks for itself. I fear that his present job means never-ending work as the battery will have to serve the Division and battalions come and go from the trenches but the Division is there all the time. However, he may have a slack time if there is a general advance. The chances of leave seem small, I fear.

Regarding yourself, I had a good look round for a shirt but there was only another old rag and a flannel shirt belonging to Hughie. Regarding pictures, I bought a few which I think are all right but it would not be wise to send them on as they might get broken. However, we will settle the question at Christmas when you come home, all being well. My friend has five Baxter prints; they are small, (about 12" square) but lovely things, quite scarce and valuable and beautifully framed. He will take £4 for the lot if they are anything in your way. You might try some of the picture shops in Dublin and ask if they have any Baxter prints and send me the particulars, i.e. subject, size, condition, if framed

---

[47] See bibliography

or not and price. I think the prints my friend has quite a bargain but I do not want to buy any more pictures myself.

We were sorry to hear about Neuendorff. We are glad you like Dublin and doubtless it will be more pleasant in summer. We are going to Lowton on Saturday, all being well. Nothing fresh here at present. We are both quite well. How is your health? You do not say. Love from both, your affectionate Father.

GW: *I was settling into Trinity College at this time. Neuendorff was a German schoolmaster who had been an assistant to me in my last year at the Manchester Grammar School and had coached me for Entrance Scholarship to Cambridge. He and his wife received me as a paying guest in their flat at Bismarckstrasse 10, Charlottenburg, during the winter of 1910-11 when I was a student in the University of Berlin. He was killed on the Russian front in the first weeks of the War. My own letters to my parents from Dublin have not survived. The other letters from them in 1915 are dated Oct. 28th, Nov 2nd, Nov 6th, 9th, 13th, 18th, 24th and 27th. They contain only trivial day-to-day occurrences and generally accompanied the latest letter from my brother Hugh, stuck in the trenches in France. I quote a few extracts only.*

October 28th, 1915: Mother to Gilbert

One couldn't help feeling sorry about Neuendorff with you having been a member of his household. How his poor wife and children must feel it; one can only feel sorry.

November 13th, 1915: Father to Gilbert

It is remarkable how the War Office conducts its business; however, they have settled the thing for you this time, perhaps something suitable may yet turn up for you.[48] Meanwhile I suppose you are rubbing up your Serbian. The information re MacRury is interesting. You and he would make a strong combination. He might do something for you. It is remarkable but nevertheless a fact that for one's own advancement, given the necessary qualification even as in your case, how dependent we are upon other people's recommendation for an opening.

GW: *Evan MacRury had been at Gonville and Caius when I was at St. John's College. He was a native of South Uist and rather older than the average in my year. He was very much of a lone traveller and by 1912 had visited several of the Balkan States, especially Albania. When I planned my Serbian tour in that year we arranged to meet at Spalato (now Split) and we travelled together by steamer to Ragusa (now Dubrovnik). I disembarked there and he*

---

[48] This probably refers to the fact that Gilbert was turned down for military service on account of his poor eyesight.

went on to Cattaro and Albania. When the War began in 1914 I rather think he became involved in Military Intelligence and it may have been him who put my name before that department in November 1915, or it may have been the result of my own initiative. Anyway, I found myself in the War Office and was interviewed by a Mr. P. and by Sir E. Denison Ross, the Orientalist. Then I was asked to wait in another room and then to my astonishment, in walked a Miss B…, whom I had known in Leipzig as a student of music. "Hallo," said I, "what are you doing here?" "Oh," she said, "somebody knew I had lived in Germany and recommended me for a job here. Actually, it's my job to report on all applicants for German appointments." "Are you going to test my knowledge of the language?" said I. "Well, yes, I know it's silly but I have to." Thereupon the embarrassed Miss B. produced half-a-dozen letters in German script of varying degrees of legibility. I studied the more difficult specimens and then read them out to her. "I don't know how you do it," said she, "that one took me three weeks." "What happens now?" said I. "Well, I have to report to Mr. P." said she, "and then I suppose he'll see you again." So Miss B. departed and presently Mr. P. came in. "Well, of course, your German is very good," said he, "but we don't seem to have a suitable vacancy. We might want somebody for Serbian sooner or later." I had indicated at some stage that I had a beginner's acquaintance with that language, so it was agreed that I should go back to Dublin and continue my Serbian studies. In ten days or so I did actually receive a summons to report to the War Office for a post in the Balkans but the notice was far too short and I refused on the grounds that I did not yet feel competent. By the time I had made reasonable progress, Serbian resistance had collapsed and the War Office lost interest. My real chance came in mid-November, 1917, when I received an invitation from Admiral Hall, prompted by my colleagues E.C. Quiggan and L.A. Willoughby, to enter the Naval Intelligence Division, in which I served as Lieutenant R.N.V.R. until January 1919.

November 24th, 1915: Mother to Gilbert
It was quite good to read of Redmond's visit to the front and the good feelings towards both Dublin and Ulster soldiers who are fighting side by side.

February 18th, 1916: Mother to Gilbert
Grandfather came last Sunday, looking as bright as a button and quite amiable. "God-blessed" us all when he departed and hoped both you and Hughie would soon be able to go and see him. He thought he wouldn't be much use at the front unless he could go and pot them from a barn!

John Jackson was then 91, had evidently walked the three miles from his home at Hebers and was about to walk back. He died in November 1919.

February 26th, 1916: Father to Gilbert
I hope that your endeavours re ousting German professors and books from our schools and colleges will have good results and I have no doubt that you will put all your usual energy into the job and it is quite as important and necessary as

fighting them in the field of battle, indeed you are better equipped than most folk for this business and in doing it, in my opinion, are doing your share of your country's work. I know you must feel out of it in not being on active service but do not let that trouble you as your eyesight disqualification is fatal to that course whereas in other matters you do count.

GW: *This refers to a small organisation of British University teachers I formed with the objective of ensuring that, after the War, British students, not German immigrants, should be appointed to our chairs of German and that British, not German text-books should be made available. Robertson consented to be Chairman, I acted as Hon. Secretary, and Sandbach of Birmingham, Gough of Leeds, and Smith of Glasgow all helped. We had a meeting in Manchester but I did the business by circulating members. After Sandbach, when Gough and I entered the Admiralty contact became easier. Willoughby and Quiggan were already there. Frank Tiarks, Lieut. Commander, son of Henry Tiarks, helped us with a gift of £500 to finance a series of publications by British scholars. After the War, British scholars were given practically all the senior academic posts in German that came vacant or were newly created and our little organisation quietly expired as the need for it ceased.*

March 17th 1916: Father to Gilbert

I am glad to hear that the O.T.C. is getting more interesting to you, also that you had an article accepted in *The Times* Literary Supplement. The anti-German professorial campaign is quite your business and you are committed to make it go and if successful it will be a great national work. Someone has to do a lot for nothing at first but doubtless you would be in at the division of the spoils.

March 24th 1916: Mother to Gilbert,

I hope you have kept clear of the rebel regiment. It is rather disquieting news but I am looking forward to seeing you at home to-morrow week.

I must have mentioned seeing Sinn Feiners drilling or manoeuvring. I certainly remember, one day while out with the Dublin University O.T.C., seeing a man openly wearing a green uniform.

March 25th, 1916: George Wadsworth[49] to Helen[50]
Y.M.C.A. H.M. Forces in Egypt. Mediterranean Expeditionary Force

Dear Cousin Helen,

Just a line to let you know that I have arrived in France and was glad to get away from the sand of Egypt. Two weeks ago I sent you a photo of myself and my mate but I did not send the address for I forgot to. I had a good trip from Egypt, there were a thousand of us on board. I have had two letters from Mrs. Gibbs since I have been over here and she is quite well and so are the rest. I met a brother of mine in Egypt that I have not seen for twelve years. I hope this finds you well as it leaves me. Write soon.

I remain, Your loving friend, George A. Wadsworth.

April 20th 1916: George Wadsworth to Sarah Helen
France

Dear Cousin,

I received your letter the other day, but was very busy and didn't answer it. I had a letter from Arthur yesterday and he got your letter all right. We are getting away from the place we were in but I think that it will be a hotter place than we were in and a fishing boat will take us back. Would you send me some shaving soap and cigarettes for our allowance has been cut off and we cannot buy them here. I have not heard from New Zealand for a long time now. I do no think that they have been getting all my letters. I have not got much news just now so I will close hoping that this finds you well as it leaves me the same.

I remain, your Cousin George

April 20th, 1916: Father to Gilbert

I see from the papers that the "Sinn Feiners" have been having a fright in Dublin and appear to have been preparing a "Sham Fight" which did not come off. They are a weary crowd. I should imagine that the term "Sham Fighter" would about set them up with a truly descriptive name and one to be understood by the people. I expect they will be dealt with when the war is over.

---

[49] See Appendix for Wadsworth family
[50] Helen Gibbs, Belle Vue Place, Port Chalmers, N.Z.

GW: *This looks as if my father was referring to the arrest of Roger Casement. My mother wrote the first half of the letter and dated it April 20th. My father then added two pages. John McNeill's proclamation "cancelling the manoeuvres" was not published, I think, until Sunday, April 23rd.*

April 24th, 1916: The Irish Rebellion
Letter written by Lieut. G Waterhouse, Dublin University O.T.C., to a friend in Manchester May 1916

The affair began, of course, on Easter Monday and the first sign I had was the sound of heavy firing to the south of the College. I was working in my rooms at the time and although the shots sounded very close I put them down to a field-day which I knew the Volunteer Defence Corps (Loyalists) were to hold in the neighbourhood. In fact, our Adjutant, Major Harris, had gone away about 10 a.m. to take charge of them. Our C.O., Major Tate, had also left about 9 a.m. for a holiday in the north and he was unable to get back for a week. As the other officers of the contingent were all busy on their various business premises in the city, I was the only one left in College at the time.

The firing went on intermittently from about 11 to 1 o'clock but, as I say, I took little notice of it. When I turned out for lunch, however, I met one of the Fellows, who told me that the Sinn Feiners were out and had occupied St. Stephen's Green and were entrenching. I thereupon hurried down to our headquarters, which are at the Westland Row end of the College Park, and found the usual guard of three men and a corporal. He had already closed and locked all the gates, so I returned to my rooms to change into uniform and collect what men I could. At half-past one I went down again with two or three junior officers of various regiments, who had drifted in, and two or three men. By this time we mustered perhaps a dozen, and I at once barricaded all gates leading from the premises, which were luckily enclosed by a high wall. All this time the rebels were in possession of Westland Row Station, about fifty yards away, and of the railway viaduct, which overlook our headquarters. As we had 300 rifles and much ammunition, we could meet an attack at any moment but not a rebel showed himself. I suppose they thought us stronger than we were. They occupied the premises of the College of Surgeons' O.T.C. on Stephen's Green, but the bolts of the rifles had been removed, so they got little there.

During the afternoon men of various regiments drifted in for safety and I armed them as they came. By 3 o'clock a captain arrived and took over the command. By nightfall we had 40-50 men and were on watch all night. We learnt by signal from a friendly house that an attack was threatened about dawn but nothing came of it. At an early hour it was decided to evacuate the O.T.C. building, which was overlooked on all sides, and to move our stores in to the main buildings of the College. A small party was sent to the Front Gate and they killed one rebel and wounded another, about 4 a.m., capturing three cycles, three rifles, and 2000 rounds of ball ammunition. Until dawn I was occupied with a fatigue party conveying rifles and equipment from headquarters to the College.

By six we had made a clean sweep of everything and occupied the front block of the College buildings and the roof, which commands the main streets for about a quarter of a mile in every direction.

The whole of the day and the next night I spent with a party of snipers on the roof. We cleared all the adjacent roofs of enemy snipers and kept College Green, Grafton Street, and Westmorland Street clear of the enemy, and we were also able to fire on them in the Mail and Express Building and Sackville Street. Our front windows were sandbagged and bristled with rifles, mostly Drill Purpose. We learnt, however, that a bullet from a D.P. did not stray very far from the mark at short ranges. A few bullets came our way but we had no casualties.

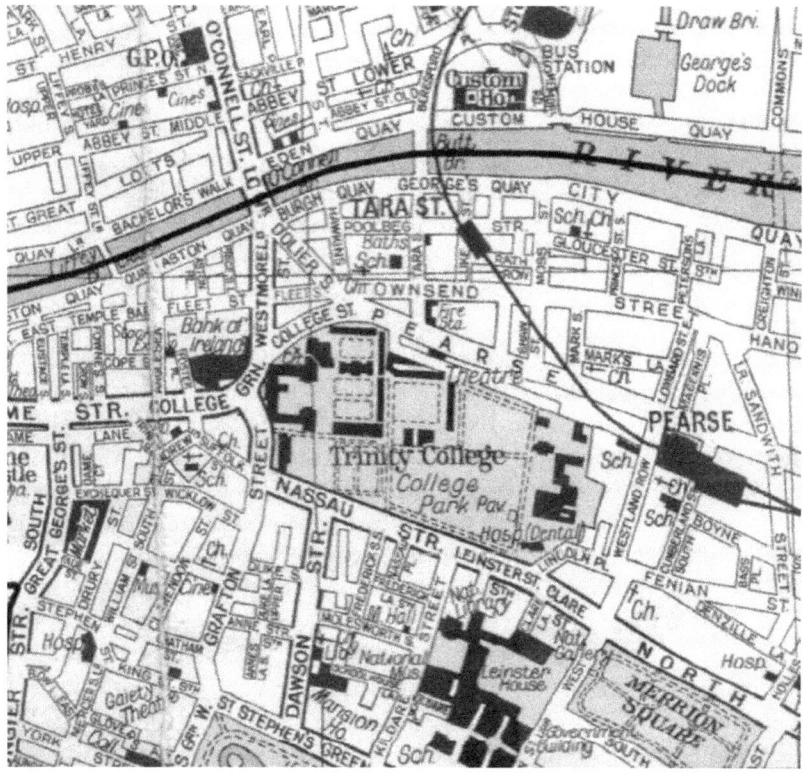

About 5 p.m. on Tuesday we were relieved by a battalion of the Leinster Regiment, which had come up from the Curragh, and had cleared the rebels out of the City Hall and the Mail and Express Building. For the next few days we had a couple of thousand troops in the College. On the Wednesday, Liberty Hall, one of the strongholds of the rebels, was knocked to pieces by artillery and steps were taken to surround them in other parts of the city. The rebels held practically all the buildings in Sackville Street and the chief shops were looted by them or their hangers-on and then set on fire. Half the street was ablaze on the Wednesday night and was an extraordinary sight to us on the College roof.

On the second or third day, while I was on the roof with a party of men looking down Dame Street for signs of the enemy, one of the College Porters came clambering over the tiles. He handed me a letter, which I opened and read: "Dear Waterhouse, Will you kindly conduct the V. V. Examination in French (Pass for Junior Freshmen) at 2.30 this afternoon? Yours sincerely, W. Westropp Roberts, Senior Lecturer." I duly donned my gown over my uniform and examined the enterprising candidates who had ignored all the hazards of the streets to reach the Examination Hall. I handed in my results at the office, took off my gown, and returned to my post on the roof.

The next day I was made Acting Intelligence Officer and spent my time examining prisoners – and filthy scum they were. They were all in civilian clothes but some carried revolvers and ammunition. Of course, when they saw the rebellion was fizzling out, the majority would throw away their weapons and pose as peaceful civilians. Most of those I had to deal with found their way to the Castle. On the Saturday morning, about 60 refugees came in, saying they were fleeing from their burning homes, etc. I had the men searched and found half of them – and women too – laden with loot from the shops. One woman had £80 in gold, a man £45, another man, about 50 threepenny bits. Another man had a canvas bag with "Royal Mint" stamped on it. Another had thrown away a revolver behind the railings of the Bank of Ireland and was betrayed by a fellow-culprit.

The woman with the gold said, I think truthfully, that the money was her savings. We persuaded her to deposit it in one of the banks on College Green.

On the Saturday afternoon I was sent over to the Custom House with about 40 men, to guard about 250 prisoners and 200 refugees. The former were the lowest of the low. Nor were many of the refugees above suspicion. It was another sleepless night for me, as one of my officers collapsed from overwork and I had to take his duty. During the night a prisoner in one of the dangerous cells went mad and I was sent for. It took three of us to hold him and tie him up.

We were relieved after 24 hours by a detachment of cavalry and returned to College, where I was put on to censor letters for a time. Then we began to send out house-searching parties. It was rather exciting work but we found little. Of course, it was too late, as the guilty parties would naturally take steps to destroy incriminating evidence when they saw there was no hope for the rebellion. Still, one or two important arrests have been made.

During the latter part of the second week I was appointed Deputy to the Assistant Provost

Marshal and was concerned principally with prisoners and the issue of passes. Yesterday the O.T.C. was inspected by General Maxwell; Mr Asquith was also present.

All the banks round College Green say the O.T.C. saved them and they are going to make some presentation. This is the only O.T.C. that has ever been in action and I feel that I am very lucky to have had a share in the business. Everything is quiet now and I have not heard a shot for a couple of days. The public is delighted with martial law and hopes it will last. Respectable people can carry on their business and the agitator has no chance.

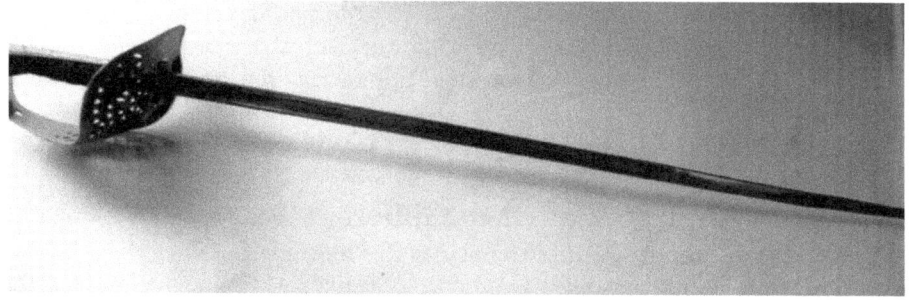

Inscription on sword reads:

Presented by the Citizens of Dublin to
Lieut. G. Waterhouse
in commemoration of services rendered by the
University Officer Training Corps
during the
Sinn Fein Rising Easter 1916

April 26th, 1916: Mother to Gilbert

Father and I are anxious to know if you took any harm through the riot on Monday.

April 28th, 1916: George Wadsworth to Gilbert France[51]

Dear Cousin, I received your most welcome letter yesterday and was very pleased to hear from you. I am in the north of France just now and it is very wet compared to what we have been used to and I have got a bit of a cold but I am getting used to the cold weather now. I have had several letters from home and they are all right in New Zealand. We have to write our letters on our knees and cannot write too well, so you will have to put up with the writing all the same. I have not much to say just now so will close hoping that this finds you as it leaves me.

I remain your Friend, Geo Wadsworth

April 29th, 1916: Father to Gilbert

We received your short note dated Thursday this morning and were thankful that you are safe. The outbreak seems to be quite futile and doomed to failure, the only fear is that so many useful lives are being lost. I see that two 2nd Lieutenants have been killed, poor boys. The situation appears brighter this morning and we may hope to see the rising put down in a few days, I think.

May 4th, 1916: Mother to Gilbert

I got your two most welcome letters yesterday morning, Wednesday, and this is the first time I have had time to answer them. Father and I have been indeed thankful to hear of your safety during this terrible uprising, our anxiety was very great and not without cause.

May 12th, 1916: Father to Gilbert

Things in Ireland are bad judging by this morning's paper. Englishmen's lives and soldiers' lives do not appear of much account to men like Dillon, whereas any little Irish guttersnipe can be almost a glorified angel. It is very extraordinary.

---

[51] The letters typically say "Somewhere in France" or "Somewhere in Belgium," that being all that was permitted.

June 1st, 1916: Mother to Gilbert

Have you seen your name figuring in Wednesday's Dispatch about the doings of the O.T.C. in Dublin which has been taken from "Ulula"?[52] Mrs. Groves[53] has been today and read it. Her own relations out there were between the rioters, and a gentleman neighbour went to try to save his shop from being looted and was shot down dead and buried in his clothes. He had been saved from the "Lusitania."

Mrs. Groves' own relatives never went to bed for 5 nights, with no light, but came through unharmed fortunately. Both she and her brother were very glad to hear that you had come through safely.

One of the men in Hughie's battalion was over in Heywood last week and he told Mr. Clare and others in a public place that it was Mr. Waterhouse who ought to have had the V.C. never mind the M.C. as it was he who did the most, and all the men thought well of him.

GW: *This refers to an incident on night patrol on Christmas Eve, 1915, when my brother and a corporal carried back a wounded man. Hugh recommended the corporal for gallantry and got him the D.S.M. It was not until the last days of the War, at Ath in November 1918, that he received the M.C. himself.*

June 4th, 1916: George Wadsworth to Sarah Helen No.26/647 France

Dear Cousin,

I received your letter but I have not got your parcel yet. I have just come out of the trenches for a spell after being in for ten days, it was very quiet up there and I had a good time and plenty of duck for dinner, this is life when you see shells landing about ten yards off you, a man did not know he was alive until he came here. You may get a service card while I am in the trenches we cannot write letters there. I did not get any letters from New Zealand this mail I think it was lost somewhere in France. A balloon of ours broke away the other day and went over our lines to the enemy lines and the two of them came down in a parachute.

---

[52] Ulula was the magazine of the Manchester Grammar School of which Mr. Paton was Headmaster.
[53] A neighbour with relations in Dublin – see photograph

One landed safe and the other got hurt but we did not see the balloon again. I will now close hoping this finds you well as it leaves me. I remain, your Cousin George

June 6th, 1916: Father to Gilbert

I was afraid Mr. Paton had outstripped your wishes in the matter of the O.T.C. defense of Trinity College, Dublin, and the United Kingdom but cheer up. It pleased your Mother and me, also some others besides us. The Prince of Wales has received the Military Cross, why should you not be recognised? As you remark, newspaper men have a faculty of going up the wrong street, so to speak… Reverting to the Dublin University O.T.C. dear old Paton was anxious to give you a boost and by Jove he's done it.

July 7th, 1916: Mother to Gilbert

I find that, all being well, you expect to be at Chelsea from Monday 10th.

GW: *This refers to a special course of instruction for Infantry Officers at Chelsea Barracks which I took in order to qualify for promotion to substantive rank as Lieutenant, being only temporary Lieut.*

Letters to Mrs. Sarah Helen "Nellie" Waterhouse

August 4th 1916: Arthur Wadsworth
France

Dear Cousin,
Just a few lines hoping this will find you all in the best of health as it leaves me at present. I had a letter from George the other day, the first for a month. He is only 16+ miles away from me but as we are not allowed to put the names of places in letters we cannot tell one another where we are. I was getting worry about him and then I saw a New Zealand boy who does the transport work up where he is and he said that the Battalion had been cut about so I gave him his address and a day or two after I got his letter. I felt more satisfied but if the other fellow sees him he will tell George where I am camped. Things have been pretty quiet on our front there the last few days, they must be welcoming the New Year or getting ready to. I wish they were getting ready to make peace and let us get back to the land of milk and honey

We are having great weather here so far, not as hot as it was in the land of sand, flies and sore eyes. Of course that place is Egypt – we were not sorry when we had seen the last of that place. Just fancy I have been away from N.Z. six years and it was the first time in twelve years when I met George in Ismailia, Egypt,. I went to his camp on the Friday and he came up to me on the Sunday and about Thursday he left for France but I have not seen him here yet. By the English papers you are having some heat waves over there.

It makes us laugh when they say a heat wave 84 deg. in the shade because when we have a heat wave in Australia it is 107 deg. in the shade and sometimes more. Well, I think I will draw this letter to a close in case I run out of news for the next one.

With love to all I remain your cousin, Arthur Wadsworth.

September 17th, 1916: from Mother

I had a letter from New Zealand on Friday with an article that a New Zealander[54] had written who was in Trinity College at the time of the Rebellion saying what a lot of sleep was lost in defending the College, Bank, etc. much the same as you wrote us.

September 23rd, 1916: from Arthur
France

Dear Cousin,
Just a few lines hoping this will find you all in the best of health as it leaves me at present. I have been waiting this long time for a letter but as my address was crossed out on other letters I suppose it was the same with yours, but if you write to Mrs. Brooks, 51 Wood Street, Middleton Junction, Manchester[55],

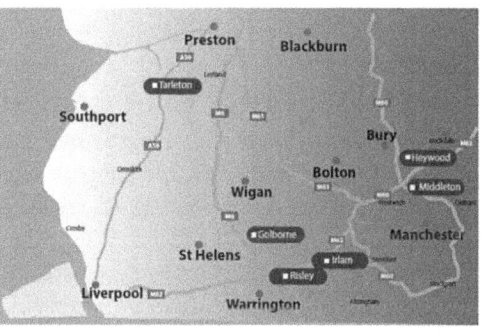

she will send it to you as George had given it to her before I had arrived in France. George is in No. 3 British General Hospital, France with a slight wound in the neck. He said he had lost the address and could not write to you so I have sent them on to him. There is plenty mud here at present but the rain has stopped for a while. We are expecting to get furlough about the middle of next month or the end.

I think this is all the news this time so I will close now with love to all.

I remain yours sincerely, Cousin Arthur.

---

[54] Was this Cadet Cpt. Don Malcolmson, NZA or Private Waring, 6th NZ Infantry or L-Cpl. McLeod, 2nd NZFE? See Sinn Fein Handbook, Chapter V - The Irish Rebellion April 24th, pp. 17-18 & p.214.

[55] This refers to the family of Sarah Helen's uncle John Wadsworth who lived at Hebers, nr. Middleton Junction. Mrs. Brooks was a neighbour.

September 29th, 1916: from George
3rd British General Hospital, Trepot[56]

Dear Cousin,

I am still in hospital and am doing well. I think it will not be long before I am back in my Battalion if any is left. Our boys got a good doing when they helped to take Flers on the 15th and 16th of September and they were in the counter attack from the Huns so I do not think there is many left by now. We may go back to Egypt for the winter, there is a lot of our boys gone over there from here and I am getting one of my mates to take this with him and post it. I wish I was going with him too and see something of the old Country before I go. I do not think much of the hospital I am in and don't think they care much for us. I got better fed down the line than I get here. The mate of mine that is coming over has got a hit in the leg and I will give you his address. Private Acourt, 2nd Otago Battalion, 8th Company, 2nd Infantry Brigade, New Zealand Forces. I wish you would send some of the addresses of the others, I have left them all behind in my cart. I never had to make a row until I came and I have been used to rough life before. I will be here for a few days yet. I will close hoping you are as well as I hope to be soon. I remain, Your Cousin George.

October 11th, 1916: from Mother

All the letters we wrote to Hughie from Llamfairfechan have been returned. I was reading one of mine this morning in which I said that I had been dreaming he was in England. How strange to realise how many of my longings and dreams have come to pass. I do feel that God has heard and heeded my prayers. Hughie left this morning for Oswestry where he is to have a month and then another medical board so we must be thankful that he has so much in his favour - although the war looks as though it would last a long time yet... Father is not very well nor am I, but as there are still a few days holidays yet we may spend them at Blackpool. Poor old Father, it's time he eased off a bit, I'm thinking. I don't think somehow we will stay at Heywood much longer. I have just about had enough of it.

October 29th, 1916: from George
France

Dear Cousin,

Just a line to let you know that I am back in the trenches. I was not sorry to get out of the hospital and get back with my mates, that is not saying that I like the trenches, no one can say that he likes this life. I lost a lot of my mates in the big

---

[56] Le Tripot, on the coast, 30km N.E. of Dieppe.

go and I hope I am not in any more like that one. I did not get back to the driving but I am with a Lewis machine gun so instead of putting Driver it will be Rifleman. I can't tell you how they are doing at home for I have not got any mail for two months, it all went to England when I was in hospital. Arthur went down to the place that we were in last month and I think that he will be getting something hot too, he may get something that will take him home to England. I hope that you got my photo and letter all right that I sent from hospital. I have been back about ten days now and am settled down to that life again. I cannot find much more news so goodbye. I am in the best of health and I hope you are the same.

I remain, your loving Cousin, George

November 12th, 1916: from Arthur
France

Dear Cousin Helen,

Just a line hoping this will find you all in the best of health as it leaves me the same at present. I wrote a letter some time ago and do not know if you have received it or not or if you got my correct address which you can get from Mrs. Webb[57], Strathgona, Bramhall, Cheshire, as I think she said you were her sister. We have been on the move and the N.Z. took over our last front. We were down where the mud was knee deep but are back twenty odd miles now in a rest camp, but will be back in the mud again before long. I thought this time last year that it would be sure thing we would be back in Australia this Xmas and only six weeks to go we will not be back there, I don't think any Blighty either but we shall be somewhere in France for Xmas Day. I think this is all the news this time – hoping to hear from you soon. I will close with love to all, I remain your loving Cousin Arthur

November 17th, 1916: from George
France

Dear Cousin,

I received your letter and was very pleased to hear from you. I received your last letter all right. I will be on this line for some time until the winter is over and then

---

[57] "Auntie Jenny" to Gilbert and Hugh. Jenny Webb, née Jackson, was Sarah Helen's younger sister.

we will be moving about pretty often so if you send anything over now it will be all right. I have got plenty of socks and mitts and do not require them, but I would like you to send over some cigarettes for we do not get a great deal of money to buy them. We had to leave 3 shillings of our pay back in New Zealand. I had a letter from Mrs. Gibbs the other day and she seemed to have had a knock when she heard that I got wounded but I told them that I was not worth worrying about. I will be going back to the trenches again in a day and will be in a few days. I will close hoping this finds you well as it leaves me.

I remain your loving Cousin George

November 27th, 1916: from Arthur
France

Dear Cousin Helen,

Just a few lines to let you know that I am still alive in this whale of a place but nevertheless I hope this will find you all in the best of health as it leaves me the same at present. We have moved back again to help to do our own little bit against the Hun. The night we arrived here it was dark so we had to get through the mud the best way we could and get our blankets and make our beds under a rape fence in the mud, my mate and myself, but we awoke in the morning to find our blankets were covered in frost. The following night we found a dryer spot but still out in the open, but now we have a dugout made out of iron the shape of a tank mat in the ground.

This is some country sure I wish I had never seen it. The place where we were before would have done me but we have all got to have a taste of the bad places. The mud makes things worse than what the job really is. We get a few shells here every day but most of them duds.

I think I will have to draw to a close as my feet are wet and cold, so bed the best place. I wish you all a Merry Xmas and a Happy New Year for we are all doing our best to have the same over here.

I remain your loving Cousin, Arthur

December 3rd, 1916: from Arthur
France

Dear Cousin Helen,

Just a few lines hoping this will find you all in the best of health as it leaves me the same at present. I received your welcome letter the other day dated Sept. 17th, it has been a long time on the way and has been all through the Army here in France. This is the first letter I have received from you, the first one has not reached me yet. I know where the worst part of the line is because that was where George got his wound. I hope you have heard from him by this. I never write to any of my Aunties in N.Z. They never write to me and I have not got their address, only Auntie Bessie, she wrote to me a few weeks back. I do not like writing but of course if they were to write to me I would certainly answer their letters but they do not trouble me so I do not trouble them. I think that this is all the news this time, I will close with best of health to all. I remain yours sincerely, Cousin Arthur.[58]

December 6th, 1916: from Arthur
France

Dear Cousin,

Just a few lines hoping that this will find you all in the best of health as it leaves me at present. Your letter to hand dated Nov, this is the second letter I have ever received. I am in the Australia forces, not New Zealand. We are back in the mud again and it looks as though we are going to be here for Xmas but I hope not. This (Fifth Australian Divisional Train) are having a very rough time. It is very hard to get things we need here as we see villages that used to be. I had a letter from George the other day, he was well and doing a bit of cooking. I had a rather big mail last night, three letters from N.Z. Leave is working around my way but I think it will be after New Year before I get to England. I am anxious to see my great uncle at Middleton. I hope that Mr. Waterhouse is quite well again and it will not be long before I can pay you all a visit as the days seem to fly. It will take many years to forget all about the hardships we have gone through. I think this is all the news at present, I will close wishing you a merry Xmas and a Happy New Year, "Twenty-eighth Australian Army Service Corps."

I remain your affec. Cousin, Arthur

December 6th, 1916: from George
France

Dear Cousin,

I received your parcel and I was very pleased to hear from you, I am out of the trenches today and it is very cold. I hope your husband is well by the time you get this and I will write again when I receive the parcel. I will close hoping this finds you well as it leaves me the same.

Your loving cousin, George

---

[58] Picture 37

December 12th, 1916: from Arthur
France

Dear Cousin,

Just a few lines hoping this will find you all in good health as it leaves me likewise. I received two letters from England today, one from you dated 5th December and Bramhall same date. I got Cousin Jenny to send me over a pair of gum boots and I will not be sorry when they arrive as we are badly in need of them to get about in this slush as our other boots will not keep out the water.

During this morning snow began to fall and everything was covered in a very short time but as the ground was not frosted beforehand the snow soon melted making the place terribly sloppy.

Our latest experience was to be woke up at half past one with mud falling in all directions caused by one of Fritz's shells bursting a few yards away. It was a very trying time for the next hour expecting at any moment for one to land in our dugout.

As we lay and listened to them coming over a big lump of mud fell on a tent and knocked it half in but we had to laugh – one lad in the dugout behind us said that it was dirt falling off the shell and if they did not come any closer we would win. Some in the tent started to sing "We want to go home." One cannot realise what it is like only those who are there. I had a look at the shell hole it was about six feet deep.

As news is very scarce I will close and will drop a line as soon as the parcels arrive, love to all, I remain your affec. Cousin Arthur

December 27th, 1916: from Arthur
France

Dear Cousin,

Just a few lines hoping this will find you all in the best of health as it leaves me in a better humour than I was on Xmas Day. I have been going to write this long time but have been putting it off. Your parcel arrived here quite safe and we all enjoyed the cake for Xmas tea, and the cigarettes and I must thank Mr. Waterhouse and yourself for being so good as I was quite out of smokes at the time they arrived.

We had a very merry Xmas although only had bread and cheese for dinner, a bad start we made but not a bad finish, as we had only arrived here on Xmas eve and was not quite settled down. It is a treat to be away from the big guns that we used to be up alongside and also to be out of the mud as it is not so deep down where we are.

I cannot say how long we will have to spell this time but some say it is for a month and I think the poor horses need it more than we do.

I think I will close with love to all and hope that the boys are quite safe.

I remain, your affec. Cousin Arthur

January 30th, 1917: from Cousin Bessie Bell
Sawyer's Bay, New Zealand

Dear Cousin Helen,

I received your very welcome letter and we were very pleased to hear from you but I have had no opportunity to reply until now. I have been busy all the holiday with visitors, my home is at the seaside and it is a nice change from the town. I have my brother's two children stopping with me just now but school reopens next week and then it will be everyone to his post then.

We are having beautiful weather just now very hot at times but we can do with a lot of it. I suppose you are in the cold winter I know the poor boys at the Front are. I had a letter from my nephew Arthur this week he was saying they had plenty of dirt and rain to put up with, I hope they will soon have a change. He has not been lucky enough to get leave yet or when he last wrote to me in Dec. but I hope before this he has been home to England to see you all. I know you will be kind to him, they always write and tell me about the letters and parcels they receive from you all. I do hope your two dear boys are safe and well and with God's help they are spared to you both. We have very few men left in Sawyer's Bay. You may have noticed from the paper where Bombardier G.C. Mains has been awarded the Military Medal for bravery in the field and also one of the group to be presented to the London Art Gallery (?) There are five of his family at the front and four of others and in some homes their only sons. I feel sorry when it comes to the last one, I have another friend I am just writing to tonight he has won the D.S.O. I am sending him your address and if he comes to England he may call and see you. He has two other brothers fighting and his sister's husband. They had no men left at home at all .

Hoping again all our boys are keeping well, I remain,
Your ever loving Cousin, Bessie Bell

January 31st, 1917: from Mother

We heard from Hebers about a fortnight ago that one of the New Zealanders, George, is in hospital at Hants, England. I had a letter from one of his aunts, Bessie Bell, yesterday morning with 3 views of her house at Sawyer's Bay.

February 2nd, 1917: from Father

We were delighted to hear of your Litt.D. investiture. The scarlet robe was extra. If some of your colleagues were not aware of the honour being conferred on you it would come as somewhat of a shock to them. I should think that your "stock" has gone up considerably in the College.

That was news regarding the Rebellion! Had MacNeill turned out, the matter would have been serious for you and the four men, not to speak of Dr. Mahaffy and Co. What narrow escapes you have had, in Germany and out of it. We have indeed a lot to be thankful for.

I am keeping better I am glad to say but your mother is not so well. She is feeling the strain of the last 4 months. I see that your Irish beauties are breaking out again so take care of yourself as they would as soon murder you as not.

I had probably written to my father suggesting that the chief reason why Trinity College had escaped occupation by the rebels was that the parties detailed to occupy it had obeyed MacNeill's published order "cancelling the manoeuvres arranged for Easter Monday."

February 10th, 1917: from Father

I was in the "Don" barber's shop in Heywood, where the fussy man is, and he told me quite a fine tale about Hughie. It appears that one of his customers last Saturday night was a soldier on leave from the camp at Ripon and he was dilating on Hughie's bravery and self-sacrifice in saving his life and a number of others by dealing with a defective bomb at bombing practice. The man (Schofield), related how in releasing the pin of a Mills bomb the top part of the casting fell off and in his agitation he dropped the live bomb. Hughie ordered them all to scoot, which they did, and he quickly seized the sizzling bomb and threw it over the parapet, when it immediately exploded. The soldier was full of Hughie's bravery and coolness and declared that he saved his life and the other men's, as they simply stood still till his sharp command scattered them, and he ought to have the V.C. Schofield stated that Hughie made a report of the matter and all that make of bomb is suspect and put out for examination. I also heard the same report from a gentleman I know in the town… Mr. Barker said that Lieut. Duckworth was full of praise for Hughie's work with the battalion, his bombing of the German trenches being quite marvellous, also that his work ought to be recognised. It was very unfortunate in one way that his work was divided between the 2/5 and the Trench Mortar battery as he became nobody's man, although he had done such excellent work for both. However, he came out whole, which is worth a lot of crosses… I am feeling much better and stronger now that the work bogey is laid to rest but not quite all right yet.

February 18th, 1917: from Arthur
France

Dear Cousin Helen,

Just a few lines hoping this will find you all in the best of health and that Mr. Waterhouse is quite well again. The boys were very lucky getting home in time for Xmas but we were unlucky not getting ours before it should have stopped. If it had gone its full course I would have been back here again but nevertheless there is time enough after the War which I hope is not far off. I have had letters from

George about twice a month and I had one from him today. He is in the best of health and has not been in hospital since he was wounded last Sept. I am sending a photo of him which my brother Peter sent to me from N.Z. The frosts seem to have all gone for the present but the ground is getting very muddy again. Yes, we have read all about the submarine blockade and have followed up the paper to see what they were doing to defeat it but it seems to be a failure like everything else that the enemy seems to take on but she must be a wonderful nation to defy the world the way she is doing, but it must all come to an end sooner or later.

There is nothing that we are in need of at present, we have had plenty of cigarettes lately and should they run out then we have the pipe to fall back on for we have tobacco to burn and as for money matters we have our pockets full and nowhere to spend it but if I do want anything that I cannot get over here I will give you the pleasure as it seems that you cannot do enough for us. Geo's case is different to mine because he is in the trenches and the man who is in the trenches cannot get enough.

There was a very sad case happened here a few days ago where some of the lads just out of the trenches for a spell and living in huts had a fire going somewhere a bit the worse for drink and the fire was getting low so one went to put some petrol on the fire which exploded and set fire to the hut the boards were so dry that it caught in no time and six were burnt to death.

I will close now as this leaves me in the best of health, love to all,
I remain your affec. Cousin Arthur

February 27th, 1917: from Father

We are keeping fairly well I am glad to say and trying to keep within the ration allowance. We expect to go to Southport next week to look for a house, which is rather a job; however there is no hurry. It is very dismal reading your remarks about the disloyalty in the theatres and music halls, also of the unrest among the lower classes. I see some 30/40 ringleaders have been deported to England. I expect that if the War ends soon and in our favour the Irish question will also be settled by this businesslike Government on suitable lines.

March 3rd, 1917: from George
France

Dear Cousin,

I received your letter and the little bit of money and was very pleased to get it.

I have just come out of the trenches and it was pretty hot the time I was in and mud up to the knees but I got through alright that is the main thing. My teeth were hitting one another and shivering all the time. I have not got the last mail from New Zealand so do not know how they are at home. I had a letter from

Arthur and he was alright and is still in the same place. I will close hoping this finds you well as it leaves me.

Your cousin George

March 19th, 1917: from Father

We were very much interested in the matter of the scheme of the defence of the College and especially as to the staff accepting it in its entirety after the judicious pruning by your own officers. I expect you did the thing neatly and plainly in typewriting whereas the others would probably be written more or less badly, not to speak of inferiority in the subject matter. What I mean to convey is that neatness, briefness and legibility get noticed whereas very pearls of thought if mixed up with difficulty in reading of the same are simply put aside unread by big bugs, military or otherwise. Of course this would not happen with your own officers, which clearly shows that your plan was best. Obviously the laboratories ought to be defended owing to their exposed position. Had a party of the enemy occupied them they would undoubtedly have made it hot for the College garrison. However, it is very nice to be appreciated by those who understand. Although the officer over you rather did you in the eye by placing you in charge there.

GW: *There had been talk of another Sinn Fein rising and the C.T.O had been asked by Irish Command to prepare a plan for the defense of the College. All officers were asked for ideas and my plan included small posts in the various medical school buildings overlooking the parade ground and the College Park. All the other plans advocated the abandonment of the College Park and laboratories and concentrated all forces in the main College buildings.*
This had been the course taken in the actual Rebellion. I was however given a fair deal. Both plans were submitted to Irish Command and to my surprise and satisfaction mine was approved and the other rejected. We then proceeded to carry out the exercise and I was entrusted with the Park and Laboratories section. I remember I had a camp bed in the Anatomical Museum, watched over by the skeleton of Corny McGrath the Irish Giant.

April 11th, 1917: from Mother

We hope that nothing serious results from the rebels on Easter Monday. We read of some soldiers having been stoned and the police attacked, but I expect you were busy with your own defence at Trinity.

I went to Hebers last Friday night and found Grandfather[59] looking rather delicate but otherwise "all right as his stomach kept on acting." He also enquired about you and Hughie as to your whereabouts. When I expressed my thankfulness with regards to Hughie being in his present position, all that the old man said was "Aye," while the lady Elizabeth kept a dumb silence. She had much to say however about the "fallen heroes" and expressed concern as to whether the population or the soldiers would go short supposing there was a famine, to which I cheerfully replied that I thought the soldiers would be looked after first and that the population should all be served alike. On the whole the meeting passed off very well.

GW: Relations between my mother and her eldest sister (Elizabeth Jackson) had been strained for some time. Poor Aunt E. had been a beauty in her youth but a too scornful rejection of local admirers had left her an old maid, in sole charge of my obstinate old grandfather, first on the farm and then in very straitened circumstances in humble cottages, first in Heywood and then at Hebers, near Middleton. She wrote poems about the sons of friends, acquaintances or strangers who had fallen in battle and, according to my very touchy Mother, seemed to think that my brother and I were not real soldiers because we had failed to get killed. Poor lady, in her declining years my brother Hugh was her only prop and support.

April 14th, 1917: from George
France

Dear Cousin,

I received your letter today and was pleased that you did not send the money. It is true that Arthur is married but he has not got three in the family for he just got married before he left. It is one of the others that has three in the family. I am the youngest and the biggest. I do not want you to send the money to me for I don't know where I will be for I think that it will over the top again soon and it may go astray, but I will give you the address Driver Arthur Wadsworth, 5th Australian

---

[59] John Jackson, who was about 92 at this time but would think little of walking 3 miles into town and back again.

Drivers Train, 28th Company A.S.C., he is well by the last letter I got from him and his boys was in the big push.[60] I am back having some hard training now and have a game of football every afternoon and it is all right. I will close hoping that this finds you well as it leaves me. Send the money to him for it will be all right.

I remain your loving Cousin, George

April 27th 1917: from George
France

Dear Cousin,

I again take the pleasure in writing to you and hope that you are well. We are getting ready for the next push and I would like you to send me a little money over so that I can get something to go over the top with. I want about two pound and you can get it sent from Mr. Waterhouse for I sent it to N.Z. some time ago for five to be sent to England but it will not get to me till after the big push, so I would like two pounds as soon as possible. I have not heard from over your way for some time now. We will be in the trenches again soon. I will close hoping this finds you well as it leaves me,

I remain your Cousin, George

May 8th, 1917: from Arthur
France

Dear Cousin Helen,

Just a line in answer to your welcome letter which I received some time ago, but have not felt in the mood for writing. It must have been the change of weather, for we have had lovely weather since we were out shelling but last night it rained all night and after dinner but it seems to be clearing up now. We had our sports here last Friday and Show on Saturday but we only got second for our wagon and horses this time, but the company got two second and one first prize so we must not be greedy but let some of the others have a dip as well.

I do not quite understand why that money is for me but you can keep it there until I come over for I am not quite stoney broke yet but it will come in handy for me over there. I will not tell you whether it will be soon or not but you will know I am there when I arrive. Yes, I quite understand how you feel but your letters are always cheerful for it is nice to receive a line or two from you all as it is nice to break stillness here at times. I think I will close now as I must write a few more letters to Jenny and Lizzy. Hope that this will find you all in the best of health and the two boys still safe as it leaves me in the best of spirits at present,

I remain your affec. Cousin Arthur.

---

[60] The First Battle of Bullecourt.

May 9th, 1917: from Father

I have been to Southport several times lately and have got a bit disgusted with the place. Anything suitable is invariably £10 to £15 per annum too dear, so we are giving the matter a rest till next month. I have Barley Hall on my hands until Sept. 29th so we have plenty of time.

May 18th, 1917: from George
France

Dear Cousin,

In answer to your letter and that the money that you sent out and I was very pleased to get it. I just had letters from all of them in N.Z. and they are all right, but Auntie Nell was ill for a few weeks but is getting on slowly now and she wrote too but her hand is not too firm yet. I have been having a good time these last few days on guard and we have been cooking our own and having all the good things we can buy but it will soon be over and into the trenches we go again. That won't be so good but I will get through alright. I don't think that it will be long before we get into the next big battle only a matter of a few days now but we have to chance our luck. I hope I get a good Blighty this time so I will see you before I go home.

Arthur has not answered my letter so I don't know what he is going to do with the money so it would be better for you to keep it till you get word from him. He is still in the hot place where all the fighting is going on[61] and I am glad that I am not there but we will get our turn soon enough. I have no news only the weather's better and I hope it is the same over there. I will close hoping this finds you well as it leaves me the same at present.

I remain your loving Cousin George.

P.S. W. Peacock is over there with seven wounds so if he calls I hope you will give him a good time. I think he is sweet on one of my sisters.

May 25th, 1917: from Father

There was rather an amusing incident came to our ears whilst the King and Queen were in Manchester. Of course the Queen was presented with the usual bouquet of flowers, which she sent to one of the hospitals and as they were to pass the place later, a wounded soldier was deputed to hold it so that the Queen could see it in passing. However, she stopped her carriage and stepped out to receive it, shaking hands and saying something nice the while and sailed away

---

[61] 3rd – 17th May – the Second Battle of Bullecourt

with it, much to the bewilderment of the soldier, who immediately ejaculated, "Dammit, she's pinched it!"

May 26th, 1917: from Father

I trust that the Provost will be able to find you a decent job in the War Office, although these things are hemmed in with difficulties, still if he really does try, he can do so much more for you than you can do for yourself. I went to Liverpool, etc., with Arthur Wadsworth, and went to New Brighton and Seacombe.

GW: *(Looking at houses). Arthur was on leave, "Blighty," in England and went with Father Waterhouse house hunting in Liverpool, etc.*

May 29th, 1917: from Father

I was pleased to see the particulars of your Lecture today and trust that it will be successful in every way. It is very kind of the Provost[62] to interest himself in your affairs. Doubtless he thinks you are worthy of his notice. All the same, it must be encouraging to you.

GW: *I gave a public lecture in the College, entitled "The War and the Study of German." It was published by Hodges and Figgis.*

May 30th, 1917: from George
France

Dear Cousin,
I received your letter and was very pleased to hear that Arthur was over there on leave and I know that he would have a good time, but I think there is very little chance of me getting over for the leave is on the sway of stopping now and if it does I will have no chance until after the push. This may be the last time I will write until after the big push and if I have the luck I may write again. There is three chances [*sic*] so I will hope for the best, I will have to go into it with the best of heart. The weather is very good and I am in the best of health, hoping you all are the same so will close.
    I remain your loving Cousin George.

June 1st, 1917: from Father

---

[62] Dr. Mehaffy

The *Irish Times* arrived this morning and we were pleased to see that they had given you a very prominent position and a fairly good report, I should imagine. The subject matter is good and set forth in temperate language and should have a good effect with those in authority. The new Education Minister seems to be a live man and if you could meet him you might do something with him. You might send a copy of your lecture to Mr. Balfour, when he returns from America. I saw a report that he was an excellent French speaker, which is rather unusual for a British Foreign Minister. He might give you a job in the Foreign Office, which would suit you much better than your present business, although political life is full of ups and downs. Look at Winston Churchill - from £5000 a year to £400 as M.P. and what he can make from writing articles, etc. However, you would run some risk for £5000, doubtless.

GW: *In the summer of 1917, my parents moved into Ivy Bank, Fulwood Avenue, Tarleton, and I spent my vacation there. They had thirteen years of happy retirement there until my father died in 1930. In 1933 my mother came to live with us in Belfast, where she died in May, 1936. We all loved Tarleton. Indeed, for two years 1924-26, following the political disturbance in Ireland, my wife, daughter Margaret and I lived at Millshaw, a house opposite Ivy Bank. I lived in Trinity College during lecture term and at Tarleton during the vacations. It was foolish panic on my part really and we moved back and settled in Killiney, close to my parents-in-law, Sir Robert and Lady Woods.*[63]

June 3rd, 1917: from Arthur
France

Dear Cousin Nellie[64],

Just a few lines hoping that this finds you all in the best of health as it leaves me the same at present except a bit of a cold in the head. I arrived back at the company on Thursday which is still in the same place we all had a rotten time on this side before we arrived at our Company One Camp. We had to stay there three days, it was just like prison there where Y.M.C.A. halls are out of bounds to all Australian troops so you see we are not loved on this side in some of the camps. I will wait and see how the photo turns out before I send over the address so if you have them you can send me one. I got your letter yesterday also four from Australia. I will draw to a close as I have such a lot of letters to write. Love to all, I remain

Your affec. Cousin Arthur.

---

[63] Who had by this time moved higher up the hill to "Marino," which is now the Australian Embassy.
[64] Cousin Helen

July 14th, 1917: from Arthur
France
Dear Cousin Helen,

Just a few lines hoping this will find you all in the best of health as it leaves me the same at present.

We are still in the same camp but are expecting a move any time now as they will not keep us here too long doing nothing. I have not had a letter from George since I last wrote. There has been good news in the papers this week since the Russians have started a fight, but we would like very much to hear about a big air raid on some of the Germans. That is the cry from all the lads over here. I think I will have to close as I was up half past three this morning and half past four every other morning. Will close, love to all,

I remain your affec. Cousin Arthur.

September 3rd, 1917: from Isabella Wadsworth[65]
Northcote Post Office, Melbourne, Australia
Dear Mrs. Waterhouse,

I received your very welcome letter along with my husband's photos, allow me to thank you very much for the way you have sent them. They are very good, are they not? He looks a little bit sad on it but otherwise they are lovely. I could eat him alive when I look at his photo after two years' absence. I have heard such a lot about his people there, I am so thankful to see them take such an interest in them. The war is dreadful, I have quite a lot of relations in there. I had your letter this afternoon, one from my boy and one from my cousin who had pleurisy and trench feet, he is a lovely boy.

I am very well here, also hope you are the same. It is very lonely at times especially when there is anything special on and I cannot go. I think I have told you all I have to say so thanking you for your kindness, I remain yours sincerely, I. M. Wadsworth.

September 5th, 1917: from George
France
Dear Cousin,

I have been back a month now and think that it is about time that I have written. I have not been in too good a form for writing. When I came back I had to go into the trenches and out in a strong point and the weather was not too good and we were standing up to our knees in water for three days and I was pretty well done when I came out but they sent me back to the transport to do some driving

---

[65] Arthur's wife.

while some of the boys went out on leave so I am alright for a while now, and hope it will be for good. I have not seen Arthur yet but was only a little away from him at one time but am a long way apart now. I suppose you will have that photo of me by the time you get this. I will close hoping you are well as it leaves me at present.

I remain your loving Cousin George.

September 28th, 1917: from George
France

Dear Cousin,

I received your letter dates 9th Sept. and was pleased to hear that you were well. I have seen Arthur twice this last week and he is well and is only about two miles from where I am camped so we are close together just now. I hope that you have got a photo by this time for I have not got one yet myself. I went back to get my photo taken with Alex, everything is going well and in my favour so I hope it keeps up the same. I will close hoping this finds you well as it leaves me at present.

I remain your loving Cousin, George

October 8th, 1917: from Helen Gibbs
Belle Vue Place, Port Chalmers, New Zealand

Dear Cousins Waterhouse,

I received your very welcome letter and was pleased to hear your boys are both well so far. It is a weary time for us all. I really do not know how to thank you for your kindness to our boys. Their letters were full of how kind you had all been. The two we sent to see you had no mother for years and that is why I asked them not to stop about London. They only had us and though they were men they just did as we asked them. I believe you had Alex Duffy, we just look on him as one of the family, he always sticks by George, he is a dear boy and a good boy. We have not had news from him yet, he will be waiting to give us all the news, I hope you are none the worse, Helen, I know you do not keep well, you must never feel too sure when the boys are away. Is Hugh in France or is he in England and Gilbert, where is he? They have had their share to do, I wish it was over, we have twenty-eight there now, some of them in their fourth year. It will last till next spring I am thinking. Mother sends her love to you all and to Uncle. She says she is afraid he has beat her, she will never see ninety-two, she thinks he is just wonderful, how she would have liked father to have lived to have heard the boys' letters telling all about you, Helen. I should just have liked you to have seen her, she made us read them over and over. She is not alone now my brother Tom is living with her and I am pleased. She does not keep too well yet wonderful for her age. I always looked after Mother, she lives in a little valley and at this time of the year it is just lovely. We take half hour by the train, we go around the cliffs and the sea rolling in under us. It is a lovely run in the summer, all the motors pass Mother's door, they are dirty too. It is a lovely little town called Haitita. Have I sent you the views? I can't remember anyway I will try and get you them and send you. New Zealand, what do you think of our Maori troops? Has Mr. Waterhouse seen them? They are fine men, we have had a lot back wounded, they are dying out. There are not so many there now but they are so good hearted and nice to live among we have some near us now. They live near the heads that is where the boats come in the harbour. I shall mark this place on your views. I must thank you again for your kindness to our boys and it is just tea time. I will close with love from all. Tell Hugh and Gilbert, New Zealand will be a nice trip for them.

I remain your loving cousin, Helen Gibbs.

P.S. Arthur looks very much changed in the photo. I am looking for George and Alex. They are fighting again. I am looking for bad news any time they are in the middle of the battle again.

GW: *The following two letters were both written on 22nd Nov. 1917 on hearing that I had received a telegram from Admiral Sir Reginald Hall inviting me to enter the Naval Intelligence Service (the famous Room 40) with the rank of Lieut. R.N.V.R, and a salary of £600 a year.*

November 22nd, 1917: from Mother

We got your postcard this morning and cannot let it pass without our best wishes for your welfare and best hopes that you may you have reached the right turning point for some lasting pleasure as well as duty to your country.

I saw the new moon last night which gave me a feeling of good intent or portent. Be that as it may, I felt an immediate desire to do some good, so I made a parcel of one of my warm winter coats (a very good one but out of date) and am sending it in aid of Serbian prisoners as asked for in *The Times* yesterday. I feel I have done the right thing as people in this country seem to be short of nothing really.

November 22nd, 1917: from Father

We received your very interesting letter this morning. The position you have been offered is just "it" and we have no doubt whatever that you only require the opportunity to make your presence felt. It is rather remarkable that it has taken the authorities so long to discover you, doubtless your pamphlet on German has been the cause. It was fortunate that you seized on that opportunity and had practically the field to yourself. Doubtless lots of Johnnies are wondering why they did not undertake so obvious and necessary a work. However there is no doubt that you do deserve recognition and a position where your talents and industry can be useful to your country and pleasant and honorable to yourself. I do not think there will be much trouble in getting transferred and we hope to see you in your new togs before Christmas.

Your financial outlook is now very good. Your position at Trinity will be secure now, I have no doubt, but something good out of Ireland would suit you better and it seems likely to come on later. We are both keeping very well. Your mother looks twenty-five years old at times and I am distinctly better and stronger than I have been for some time.

December 11th, 1917: from George
France

Dear Cousin,
Just a line to let you know that I am alright and still alive. I have moved away from Arthur again but will see him again some of these days. Our boys are going into a push again soon but I will miss this one this time and I'm not sorry either for I have seen enough of it. The weather is getting more like winter every day now and I won't be sorry when summer comes again. I will close hoping this finds you well as it leaves me,
    I remain your loving cousin, George

December 20th, 1917: from George
France

I received your card a few days ago and was pleased to hear that you were well but hope Mr. Waterhouse is better. I had a letter from Mrs. Brooks saying that he was not well. It is getting winter again but I don't think it will be as bad as last for the cold. I haven't heard of Arthur for some time now and do not know how he is. I wrote to Middleton about the photo so I suppose they will send it before long. Haven't got any news yet, so I will close hoping that this finds you both well as it leaves me. It is my twenty-first birthday on the 11th December so I am getting to my third year in this war.
    I remain your loving cousin, George

December 21st, 1917: from Arthur
Belgium

Dear Cousin Helen,
Just a few lines hoping this will find you all in the best of health as it leaves me the same at present. You must excuse me not answering your letter before this, but I have had my right arm badly burnt, but it is nearly better now. We have had

a lively time since I wrote to you last. We have had two wounded and one killed in our last stunt, three wagons blown to pieces, two horses killed also six others wounded. It is a wonder we got it as light as we did. Have been back in France for nine weeks, have had plenty of moving about these last three weeks and now we have to move to another camp for the winter, so will close now as I have a lot of letters to answer.

Love to all I remain your affec. Cousin Arthur.

December 21st, 1917: from George
France

Dear Cousin,

I received your letter with the little present which was very welcome. I can tell you I have carried the letter about now till it is just about in pieces, haven't felt in any mood for writing. I can tell you being so busy and the weather being cold enough to freeze two men like me and I have let the letters build up now that I want a week to answer what I have, it is getting very near Xmas now and don't think it will be a very nice one this time but it won't much matter in these times. I haven't heard from Arthur for some time now but hope he will not be long before he gets over there again. I am about six on the list for leave again but I may not get it for some time yet. I haven't got a great deal to write about for I am on house guard now and not very far off being asleep but hope to get another letter done before I go off so will have to say good morning. I don't suppose this will reach you until after Xmas so I will wish you a Happy New Year and many happy returns of the day.

I remain your loving Cousin, George.

December 22nd, 1917: from Elizabeth Vose[66]
Barton Villas, Uttoxeter.

Dear Cousin,

I am sure you will be sadly grieved at our sad loss. Our dear boy, Tom, made the supreme sacrifice in action in France on the 18th inst. We received the terrible news on Monday last, by wire from the War Office and you will readily imagine our condition since then.

I am pleased to say that we are now becoming more reconciled to our great bereavement – but it will remain uppermost in our thoughts for a very long time to come.

We have not yet received any further information beyond the wire referred to except that the chaplain has written to say that he has laid our dear one to rest, in a cemetery reserved for British soldiers.

---

[66] née Wadsworth, first cousin of Sarah Helen

You will no doubt remember Tom visiting you about 12 months ago, when he was at the hospital in Manchester after his return from the Somme.

Eddie, our youngest boy is still out there and is quite well – we had him home for 10 days in Sept. We all hope your boys are quite well and safe. Tom told us that he had heard through a Manchester friend that Hugh was out in France again.

We should be pleased to have a line from you and hope to learn that your dear husband has fully recovered from the illness from which he was suffering so acutely when we last heard of him.

Mr. Vose and Doris join me in wishing you as happy a Christmas time as possible under the present circumstances and that the New Year will bring a brighter light to all our homes and hearths. We hope to have the company of Joe and his wife on Christmas Day. He is still in London where he has had some unpleasant experiences recently from the air raids. I must now conclude, best wishes and kindest regards to all

And remain, Yours very sincerely, Eliz Vose

December 23rd, 1917: from L. A. Willoughby
The Admiralty

Dear Waterhouse,

I understand that all arrangements have been made for your coming here almost at once. I congratulate you on obtaining a very interesting and important appointment. When I joined the staff here I had been invalided out of the army and so the question of a transfer did not arise. In your case as an officer of the O.T.C. I imagine you do not hold a commission proper and living in Ireland are not subject to the Army Authorities. I presume you gracefully throw up your duties when you think fit. Collinson who had a similar position in Liverpool also was enlisted as a private. You will be granted a commission as Lieut. R.N.V.R. in due course.

I am looking forward to your advent here within the next few days.

Yours sincerely, L. A. Willoughby

GW: *My experience in Room 40 was limited to the periods November, 1917, when I was transferred from the Army to the Navy, with the rank of Lieutenant R.N.V.R., to January, 1919, when I returned to the Chair of German in Trinity College, Dublin. On entering Room 40, my first reaction was to realise that events of vital naval significance were happening almost every minute and demanding in some form or other my – I repeat my – immediate, continuous and accurate attention, and so it was for all my colleagues. There were of course lulls in the flow of paper but every man in the team had to preserve his sense of acute responsibility as long as he was on watch. We worked round the clock in teams of two or three, according to the nature of our duties. The normal watches were 4.30 to 9.30 p.m., 9.30 a.m.to 4.30 p.m. and 9.30-p.m.to 9.30 a.m., followed by about 5 hours rest between watches. Certain senior members had day duty only and the "pundits," or more highly specialised* *members did more or less as they pleased, voluntarily immured in their dungeons by day or night and emerging only to distribute the welcome fruits of their labours.*

December 26th, 1917: from Arthur
YMCA In the Field

Dear Cousin Helen,

Just a few lines hoping this will find you all in the best of health as it leaves me the same at present. We had a great Xmas dinner, it was held in the Town Hall in this village. There was five courses and plenty of it, everybody was satisfied. The dinner was on at five. There was singing and dancing after, all was merry. I think I was the only one that was missing as I had to get everything ready on Xmas Eve and did not get to bed till one o'clock on Xmas morn, so as soon as I had the dinner cooked I went to have a lay down at half-past three and did not wake up until half-past ten, so I got up and made some toast, that was my Xmas dinner. I think that is all at present so will close,

Love to all, I remain your affec Cousin Arthur

December 28th 1917: from the Admiralty

Sir, I am commanded by my lords Commissioners of the Admiralty to acquaint you that they have been pleased to appoint you as an interpreter for duty in the Intelligence Division under the Admiralty.

While holding this appointment you will receive a salary of £500 per annum as from the date of commencing duty,

I am, Sir, Your obedient servant, V. W. Baddeley

GW: *With the Armistice in November, 1918, Room 40 more or less collapsed. The stream of paper dried up. Some of us were sent here and there on various errands. I myself attended the surrender of the German submarines at Harwich, as Intelligence Officer and interpreter.*
Then, with three other officers, I was appointed to the staff of the Naval Armistice Commission under Admiral Browning. He had lost a hand in some engagement and wore a steel hook and the story ran that if he was seen to be stroking his hook gently it would be safe to meet him, but if he were rubbing it violently it was wise to disappear. One of his maxims was "I trust nobody until I have tried him." I found him very pleasant on the one occasion when he sent for me to translate some papers in his cabin. Perhaps he had noticed that his wretched little terrier dog had bitten my ankle under the table and felt it his duty to unbend a little!

January 10th, 1918: from Arthur
France

Dear Cousin Helen,

Just a few lines hoping this will find you all in the best of health as it leaves me the same at present. Your letter to hand today, dated the 5th, I also had one from Auntie Nell Gibbs.

I am aware the little wife will be pleased to receive your letter for it will help to cheer her up. I did not mind missing my Xmas dinner as long as everybody else enjoyed it which they did. There was another big snowstorm alarm the other day so we had another snow fight but today it has nearly all gone and a little bit of mud is getting about. Last night we had some Uncle Sam soldier here playing the piano and some singing and dancing up in the hall, enjoying life as we find it.

I cannot say for sure but if the leave keeps on as it is I might be over again about the end of next month. Will close now, Love to all, I remain your affection. Cousin Arthur

February 26th, 1918: from Isabella Wadsworth
c/o Northcote P.O., Melbourne

Dear Mrs. Waterhouse,

I received your kind letter and was very pleased to hear from you and I trust that my dear Husband is still well and corresponding with you. I was very pleased to think he sent you an Xmas card. I never received one at Xmas from him. I had one before I think he must be storing them all up. I feel greatly upset to think my Dear Husband and George never received their Xmas box in time for Xmas. I sent them away in time so as they could get them. I stayed up pretty well all one night preparing them, it was not that I minded as I rather like doing those things. I feel that is all I can do for them.

I try to do my best. I feel just as you say when the hours are darkest you feel God has helped you. I feel just the same myself many a time although I go about with a smiling face. I am glad to hear George is well, I trust he will come home along with my husband and when that will be I cannot say but I trust it won't be long. I think everyone must now feel this terrible war and hope never to live to see another. I was sorry to see in your dear letter that your two boys did not see one another when on leave. I am sure it must upset you to see them. I feel I would give all I have to see mine once again.

It is just two and a half years since I kissed his loving lips which if anything should happen it must not be forgotten his last few pence he gave me I put away under lock and key. I do not know how to thank you and Mrs. Webb for your kindness. I won't forget you both. Some time or other I trust my husband's arm is better, I hope he was not burnt very much, but I think the dear boys are safer wounded although some get more than their share.

Well, Mrs. Waterhouse, I think I will have to conclude, wishing you best respects and may you see your dear boys home soon, with kind regards from Isabella Wadsworth.

March 24th, 1918: Hugh to Gilbert

Dear Gilbert,

Just a line to let you know I am still alive, although I have no news as usual. We manage to fill the week with work and games at night, and time goes merrily enough. Sundays we go fishing, but catch nothing, although the sail is always pleasant.

The 42 Div and 51st seem to have got it in the neck. The 51st always were a good crowd, I was with them at La Boiselle and they struck me as the proper stuff then. They have been singled out by the Bosch before now as their worst opponents and have the reputation of being the finest division in the British Army which is saying a lot.

Things look bad just now; but if we are any good we ought to be able to imitate the Bosch and wriggle out of it; as he did on the Somme.

We had about 4 alarms of different sorts about a fortnight ago – hope you were not responsible for any of them. Two or three were air raid warnings.

Hope you are in the pink and enjoying the work. Love Hughie

April 4th, 1918: from George
France

Dear Cousin,

I received your letter and was pleased to hear that you were all well and that Arthur had a good time. As you say my mind may change when I get over there but I don't think that I will catch the four extra days as Arthur did for I think that it will be cut down to ten again and it would just be my luck to catch the ten. I should have been over there a month ago but me being in the transport I could not get my leave the same as the ones in the line and I think it is only too right, don't you, but when I got back and I was next on the list the old Hun stepped in and spoiled me again and we are not having a picnic, I can tell you, but the old saying is that "it's the war." I don't know about doing my share in the front line I did not think we could do more than we were asked before we came over here. Well, I will have to close hoping this finds you all quite well as it leaves me at present. I am not in the line but near it as a brigade runner, that is as good as the line.

I remain your loving Cousin George

May 2nd, 1918: from George
France
Dear Cousin,
Well, I suppose it is about time I answered your letter. I have been waiting to get some news but find it is hard work.

Well, everything seems alright now and a bit quieter than they were but don't know how long, if it keeps like this I may get my chance of getting leave that won't go bad.

Arthur was quite well when I last heard from him but I don't think he is handy enough to go and see him. Alex Duffy is over there with a touch of gas but think that he is getting alright now. Well, hope this finds you all in the best of health as it leaves me at present.

I remain your loving Cousin, George.

May 13th, 1918: from Arthur
France
Dear Cousin Helen,
Just a few lines hoping this will still find you all in the best of health over there as it leaves me likewise. I don't know whether I answered your last letter or not but will make sure this time, as this is 13th May, the devil's number, so I am five and twenty and feel about thirty. The weather is lovely over here, could not wish for better. We don't get troubled with old Fritz's now we are living out in the country, one never feels comfortable living in such towns over here, so will close,

Love to all, I remain, your affec. Cousin Arthur

June 6th, 1918: from Arthur
France
Dear Cousin Helen,
Just a few lines hoping this will find you all in the best of health as it still leaves me at present. Your letter to hand dated May 30th I received this afternoon. Have not had any mail from Aunt now for some time, it is about two or three weeks since I heard from George. The weather still remains fine and very warm, and there is nothing doing on our part of the front, only a few shells come down now and then. Old Fritz has not been over this way of a night kicking up a noise with his bombs as he used to. The boys pass their lovely evenings away playing cricket, they had a win tonight 100 to 40. We were playing the Black Anzac the other night and it was as good as a play to watch them, quite an enjoyable evening.

I think this is all at present so will close, love to all, I remain your affect. Cousin Arthur

July 6th, 1918: from George
France

Dear Cousin,

I received your letter some time ago and think it is about time to answer it.

Well, we have just come back after a few weeks spell and are back up the line again but it is quiet to what we left it, but will soon get rough again.

Arthur was well when last I heard of him. My leave don't seem to be any nearer now than what it was when I came back from the last and that is twelve months since the last and some of the boys have had three but that don't matter as long as they let me see the war out. I suppose that things will liven up a bit in a while and we give the Hun all that he is looking for and a bit more soon, he has not quite socked the fight out of us. Well I have no news so will close hoping this finds you all well as it leaves me at present.

I remain your loving Cousin George.

July 13th, 1918 : from Isabella
c/o Northcote Post Office, Melbourne

Dear Mrs. Waterhouse,

I received your most welcome letter on Thursday morning also two from my dear husband's brother, also one from him. I think there must be some more of his about. I'm glad your two boys are well, I am looking forward to seeing my husband very shortly. The war is dreadful, is it not? I have had a dreadful cold this week, it is not much better today. All our doctors out here have been on strike for some time now so I cannot go to the lady doctor, I am trying to get rid of it, the weather is pretty cold here just now. I am sending you on a couple of views from Australia. I am proud of our country, also my hero. It is just on three years since he left the shores of Australia, it will be over by the time you receive this. There has been many a lonely hour for me since he left and I am sure I have lost all my smiles. I used to go about smiling but I cannot now. I think there is not a home without some dear one away. I cannot forget my last dear cousin who went from here, he had pleurisy and trench feet. I heard he was limping when put back into the trenches. He was killed a little time after but I must not complain, there are some worse off than I am. Hoping all is well with you all and that your dear sons will return to you very shortly also hope my dear husband is well. I am beginning to think I am not a married woman at all. Hoping these few lines find you well,

I am yours sincerely, Bella Wadsworth

July 21st, 1918
France
Dear Cousin Helen,
Just a few lines hoping this will find you all in the best of health as it leaves me the same at present. Your letter to hand, July 10th, I also had a line from George today, he is still in good health and might be over on leave next month. I have got quite used to not getting any letters from Blighty as I have not had any letter in answer to my last letter to Lizzie and Jennie for over two months. And none from Middleton Junction. The Hun is getting some hurry up here lately, things are very quiet on this front line here these last two days. We are quiet enjoying ourselves as best we can. I do not feel like writing tonight, so will close, more news next time, love to all,
    I remain your affec. Cousin Arthur

DD: *We do not know if George enjoyed his anticipated leave. He died on 29 August 1918*

August 13th, 1918
France
Dear Cousin Helen,
Just a few lines in answer to your letter which I received today Aug. 8th a day that will be well remembered by Australians, when they went over the top and broke the Hun's line a blow the Hun will never forget either. I was on my way back from the rest camp down by the seaside and had a very good time, and on Friday 9th was on the field from where the battle started.
    Everybody you passed had a smile, for the Australians had been let loose, they got the chance they have long waited for just to show what they could do. The Hun was frightened of them but they were not of him. I hope this finds you all in the best of health as leaves me the same. I think this is all the news so will close with love to all,
    I remain your affec. Cousin Arthur

September 16th, 1918
Y.M.C.A. somewhere in France
Dear Cousin Helen,
Just a few lines hoping this will find you all in the best of health as it leaves me the same at present. Your letter to hand today dated Sept. 9th and was pleased to hear that you had a letter from Bella and that she had sent you the news which I had asked her to send, one can always get a look at the country by picture, if they have not seen it by nature. Well, things are going pretty well over in these parts at present. I thought a few days ago that we were going to get the wet weather at

last, but these last few days have been lovely and pretty warm. I think this is all the news at present so will close as I have more letters to write.

Love to all, I remain your Affec. Cousin Arthur.

DD: *The YMCA was a refuge for the wounded. Arthur died on 6th November 1918 in the great Spanish 'flu epidemic.*

December 19th, 1918: from Isabella to Sarah c/o Post Office, Northcote

Dear Mrs. Waterhouse,
Your ever welcome letter to hand this morning along with little book I think is it very nice. Well, my dear, my grief has been unbearable lately to think that I have lost my darling husband and brother[67] after all this time. I trust that my darling husband was in the care of one of his loved ones when he passed from this world of sorrow. I would like very much to hear particulars relating to my dear husband's death and did he bear much suffering, as if they did not suffer enough at war without this terrible plague.[68] I suppose God has seen fit and has taken them both home to rest. I trust that I may meet my loved ones in the far off lands and hope it won't be too long before I be with them. I feel I have lost my dearest and best, only those who have lost know what the pain is. I would love to see my dear husband's grave. I trust that it is near some of his dear ones. I may be able to come across some of these days. One never knows – did my dear one express any wish before he closed his eyes in death? I feel too broke up to write much at present. I hope your dear boys are spared to come through alright and that you will soon have them home. Thanking you for all your kindness to my dear husband and myself, hoping to hear again from you, I remain, Yours sincerely, Isabella Wadsworth.

March 26th, 1919: Isabella to 32 Dally Street, Northcote

Dear Mrs. Waterhouse,
Your most loving letter to hand through the week. Glad to hear all are well as it leaves me the same at present. Well, dear, it seems very hard to part with our loved ones, we seem as if we cannot understand them going so young.

Poor Dad is broke up I believe over his two boys being taken. Well, dear, I hope to go to New Zealand about June or July. I am longing to meet all my dear

---

[67] It is not clear whether Isabella means "[his] brother" (George) or is referring to her own brother.
[68] Spanish 'flu epidemic of 1918.

husband's relations. I often wonder if I will ever get to England, we cannot do our dear ones that have gone any good by fretting. They have earned their eternal rest and fought the good fight. Well, dear, I had a letter from Ann Sidebottom along with yours. It is comforting getting news from you all. I miss the letters from my husband, he used to write such bright news to me. I have been on the doctor's since last I wrote to you. I had an attack of Muscular Rheumatism but I am thankful to say I was only bad a few days. We were all quarantined out here with the flu, I think it is still raging but was not as bad as New Zealand and over your way. I do hope you all escaped it over there. Give my love to all, love and kisses,

I remain yours lovingly, Bella Wadsworth

April 9th, 1919: from Father
Ivy Bank, Fulwood Avenue, Tarleton, nr Preston, Lancs.

Dear Gilbert,

On Saturday morning I received a London Times of Friday April 4th which contained the announcement of Hughie's honour, under the following heading:

Gallantry and devotion to duty in the Field
Awards to Officers
The Military Cross

Then follows the announcement (amongst others):

Captain H. Waterhouse, 2/5 Batt.Lancashire Fusiliers.T.F.

The notice goes on to say that the acts of gallantry for which the decoration has been awarded will be announced in the "London Gazette" as soon as possible.

It appears that Kathleen has been on the look-out for Hughie's honour and she found it in . of April 4th and Uncle Hugh sent it on here without remarks. I naturally concluded that it came from you and I have been expecting some word from you on the subject until I had a letter from Hugh explaining the matter.

Before reporting the matter to the Heywood Bury and local paper I would like to have the details from the Gazette. I looked at a Gazette in the Southport Library yesterday and saw the matter mentioned but without any details (as in *The Times*). The Gazette was marked "supplementary" so it may not be the real paper. Can you arrange to keep the Gazette under observation? Possibly you will amend your notice to the "Eagle" and "Ulula" by adding the heading in *The Times* which reads as follows.

"The King has been pleased to approve of the awards of the Military Cross to the following officers and warrant officers in recognition of their gallantry and devotion to duty on the Field. The acts of gallantry for which the decoration has been awarded will be announced in the London Gazette as early as possible."

All well here, it is good gardening weather now and I am having a fine time. Nothing further from Hughie. Love from both, Your affec. Father

DD: *The citation reads: Awarded for conspicuous gallantry and devotion to duty at Ath on 10/11th November 1918. The skill and ability with which he pushed his company forward resulted in the capture of two important bridgeheads before the enemy had time to destroy them. In establishing forward battalion headquarters he made several journeys over ground exposed to heavy shell fire, and finding one of his officers dangerously wounded, lying in the open, carried him to a place of safety.*

June 28th, 1919: from Hugh
Ivy Bank, Fulwood Avenue, Tarleton, nr Preston, Lancs.

Dear Gilbert,

Many thanks for your long letter.

I was glad to get away from Brussels as we had nothing to do and seemed at one time to be forgotten. However an order came through to push off at 2 a.m. so we pushed off, complete with King's colour in sackcloth. Lucky for me it was not their co colour as I was the only officer with the Cadre. We did the usual cattle truck start to Lille and slept soundly as if the war were still on. Strange how one can sleep in these conditions. Lille is rotten. Had to march for 1½ hrs from one station to another right over Lille and miles beyond. Cattle trucks again to Boulogne where they were pretty quick with us. Wired to Mayor of Bury and people that mattered. Sailed 4 days after. Troops like sardines as usual. Officers comfortable.

Left Dover special train for Crewe, where they said arrangements would be made. Arrangements for men at Dover excellent. Arrived at Crewe midnight and had to shift for ourselves. Scrambled into trains for Manchester, arrived 1.30 a.m., fixed men up in YMCA Piccadilly. Couldn't get in anywhere myself and had to doss down with the lads. (Manchester Race Week). Wired Bury next morning at 8 a.m. that we should arrive at 10.30.

Met by Band, etc. Drill Hall. Colours consecrated and presented to me by the Mayor, (all wrong but I don't suppose anyone knows any better, anyway there was no Brigadier or members of the Royal Family one intended for). Took colours and deposited them in Church. Had photographs taken and then some grub. Sent men on Leave until Tuesday and then went home.

The Reception could have been better and could have been much worse. Two old Colonels could not agree what to do the night before and forgot to a large extent to let the people know – they drifted in later on however.

Took the men to Prees Heath to be demobilised on Tuesday and so finished.

Am trying now to buy a motor bike as I shall go daft if I have to stop here and it costs so much moving about on the Railways. There is a good deal to do with regard to the Old Comrades Association and I have been in Bury the last two weekends but it costs money and now that Mr. Cox has ceased to function I can see myself being very annoyed in the near future. I did not go to Ivy's wedding, very nice of you to send her the spoons. As regards "Ulule" it will have to wait. I have got a broad-minded view of things but no money and no policy at the moment, so.

Have written Sikes and will drift to Cambridge in due course. What to do or how to do it – no very clear idea. Expect I shall be furious. At the moment am rather sorry I have left the Army, but perhaps it will wear off.

I have a lot of souvenirs in shape of shell cases, steel helmets, etc.

The garden is looking well, but it is the same every day.

From above disjointed remarks and bleats you will perceive that I am like a cat on hot bricks and don't know what to do with myself and when I do it costs money, so what is a fellow to do? I think if I get a bike it will save the situation and give me change and companionship. Well, cheeroh, Your Hughie

DD: *I find this letter very sad. My Uncle Hugh had been through thick and thin with these boys. They had been his family and in his care for four years and now they went home to their wives and families. He was left, unmarried, with his aging parents in an isolated place, no job or clear idea of what he wanted to do. My father helped him to pursue his academic career which led finally to the Headmastership of Chorley Grammar School.*

Poem written by Sarah Helen Waterhouse

"Death"

When from that sacred Throne on high!
    Almighty God proclaimed this just decree,
That all who dwell upon this earth must die,
    E'en now this call is heard o'er land and sea.

Omnipotent Power unseen! Abide with us
    Through life and Death's deep anguish dark;
We fear this foe, yea, is it not ever thus
    E'en billows now are tossing round our bark.

We perish, sink and fall, before we find
    The way that leads to Thee on high!
Through Death's dark night we leave this way behind;
    Forsake us not when unto Thee we cry.

Thou art the Rock! The shelter from the storm;
    Drench'd with Death's dew, we fain would hide
Beneath Thine o'ershadowing Wondrous Form,
    Whose Hand can hold the boundless waters wide.

Oh! Leave us not to take this path alone,
    But speak sweet peace unto us when
Our spirit rises - 'neath the azure dome
    Let not our sight behold the chasm then.

This darksome way to Heaven and Thee
    We cannot find without Thine aid!
Oh! hold us when we cross this sea;
    Let not our spirit droop and fade.

Oh, teach us how to trust in Thee,
    When round us comes the foaming tide;
Father in Heaven! May we see
    That Thou wilt ever be our Guide!

Chapter VI

Allied Naval Armistice Commission Inspection of the German Navy
Second Lieutenant Officer Gilbert Waterhouse aboard H.M.S. Hercules

During the last year of the War Gilbert had been recruited by the War Office into Naval Intelligence to interpret and break the German coded messages. This culminated after the Armistice in his travelling to Kiel, etc. to take part in the Inspection of the German Navy. This is well-documented in the official records. This document is the report that he made.

I. Wilhelmshaven

Should the British Navy be destined to act as a police force for a League of Nations, historians will point to December, 1918, as the date when it first entered on its new functions. What indeed could be more like a British policeman than the great, fat battleship which waddled into Jade Bay on the morning of Thursday, December 5th, sniffed suspiciously round the dirty dockyard and then waddles solidly on along the prescribed beat to Kiel. At her approach the Huns ceased to wrangle among themselves and tidied up the remnants of their navy for inspection, vying with one another in their desire to appear peaceable and obliging. Mutinous sailors showed temporary obedience and glum officers almost welcomed the intervention of the representative of law and order.

The outward voyage was uneventful as far as wind and sea were concerned. The sun made a feeble attempt to shine as the Hercules left her buoy and passed under the Forth Bridge and through the assembled fleet, but mist prevailed and soon every outline was lost to view. Towards morning an occasional drifting mine was sighted, visible reminders of the latent perils of war, and about eight o'clock the report of a cloud of smoke on the horizon brought the curious promptly to the deck. Then occurred a meeting unique in history. The Hercules, with her escort of destroyers, Verdun, Viceroy, Vidette and Venetia, passed at distance of a mile or two the German super-Dreadnought Konig, the light cruiser Dresden, a destroyer and two large transports, tamely proceeding to internment at Scapa Flow. The possibility of such encounters had been a vain hope with the Grand Fleet for years and few could have expected that hostile ships like these could meet and pass without a shot. But the Konig's teeth had already been drawn, and her skin sold in advance, so with her companions in shame she slunk away into the mist.

About midday another blur of smoke on the horizon resolved itself into the German light cruiser Regensburg, which was to guide the Hercules through the German minefields in the Wilhelmshaven Roads. After an exchange of signals she lowered a boat and an officer, a Warrant officer and a pilot came aboard. They were met with the usual formalities and conducted to the bridge, where they produced charts and explained the intricacies of the course to the navigating officer. Other officers were taken on board the destroyers, whereupon the journey was resumed, the Regensburg leading. Heligoland came into sight towards three o'clock. A bleak cliff dimly outlined in the fading light. A fog came up about six and the flotilla was forced to anchor outside the Jade estuary, the Regensburg being completely lost to view. Next morning the light improved sufficiently, revealing the position of the light ships and other navigational marks, and before noon the British flag was flying in the deserted roads, where the Kaiser's High Sea Fleet will never lie again.

The view from the deck of the Hercules was not impressive. About half a mile away stretched a long sea wall, above which rose nothing except the top of a flat tree-covered ridge and the spire of a distant church. At the south east end of the wall was the entrance to the vast basin in which lay the surviving tatters of the German fleet, together with three or four light cruisers and a host of obsolete torpedo boats. The task of the Commission was to see that these vessels had been disarmed in accordance with the terms of the armistice, and the details of the inspection were settled at a conference in the Hercules in the afternoon of Thursday, Dec. 5th. There was great excitement when the German Admiral's barge was seen rounding the distant breakwater and many eyes gazed discreetly through portholes and from the upper works on Admiral Coette and his colleagues, Captain Muller of the notorious Emden, and Commander Hintzmann of the Naval Staff. The deputation was appropriately received at the top of the gangway and escorted to Admiral Browning's cabin. On one side of the table sat the three Allied Admirals, with the Chief of Staff, Captain Lowndes; on the other side the three German delegates. The Admiralty interpreter took his place at the end and the remaining representatives of the Allied Powers were provided with seats round the cabin. Several conferences of this kind took place both at Wilhelmshaven and at Kiel.

During the afternoon the local Soldiers' and Workmen's Council attempted to communicate with Hercules by signal, but of course without result. It was firmly impressed on the German officers that the Allied Commission would deal with them only, though it was abundantly clear that they represented only a phantom authority. There was no further trouble with these local councils, who appear to have recognised very quickly that the only chance of a speedy peace and of an improvement in economic conditions lay in the unhindered accomplishment of the task the Commission had come to perform. During the whole stay of the British ships in German waters the Soldiers' and Workmen's Councils remained in the background and, with the occasional momentary lapses on the part of over zealous individuals, made no serious attempt to interfere, though there can be no doubt that all the arrangements made by German naval officers had to be sanctioned by the men, and could not have been carried out without their cooperation.

The actual inspection commenced on the morning of Friday, Dec. 8th, when a deputation of German officers came alongside to guide the members of the Commission to the distant landing-stage. It seemed characteristic of Germany in defeat that the most prominent figures on the quay should be a cinematograph operator and a hunchbacked photographer, dodging from one position to another in their eagerness to turn their country's humiliation into cash. The docility with which the finest ships in the German Navy passed into captivity is the most striking indication of this peddling commercial spirit. Uppermost in the German mind, even in the hour of greatest disaster, is the desire to bargain, to save something from the wreck. A navy at the bottom of the sea is hopelessly lost, a navy interned is still, to the German mind, an asset, capable of being exchanged for something else, perhaps even of redemption.

As the ships listed for inspection lay scattered over the vast dockyards, the extent and arrangement of which demanded instant admiration, the Commission split up into sections, each of which was conducted by a German officer to the units it proposed to visit. Motor-boats were in readiness at another quay close by. The walk was so short, that the few civilians in the neighbourhood, mostly labourers and school children, had hardly time to realise who we were and what was happening. There was no hostility or even curiosity in their dull, expressionless faces.

Quickly the launches sped through the oily water, in marked contrast to the general inactivity. Old hulks, long transformed into depots and offices, lay lifeless against the dockside.

On the dockside, gaunt fragments of rusting machinery lay piled in apparently hopeless confusion. Near each ship stood a little crowd of men. Some still busy with heaps of recently unloaded war material, others loafing aimlessly about. Half a dozen Dreadnoughts headed the list of ships and were the first to receive attention. The procedure was in all cases the same. The inspecting officers were met at the top of the ladder by one of the ship's officers and conducted to the ward-room, where swords and overcoats were laid aside. The technical experts were then shown to their respective departments for the purpose of satisfying themselves that the requirements of the armistice had been carried out, i.e. that certain essential parts of the guns had been removed, that all torpedoes and ammunition had been landed, in short, that the ships were unfit for service. To the eye of the casual observer the once formidable battleships appeared to be already little more than scrap iron, doomed to rust away in the gloomy waters of the dock. The few officers left on board were broken-hearted but genuinely anxious to get the painful business over and give what satisfaction they could. The senior officer on board the fleet flagship Baden, a mere lieutenant, explained that he could not provide a guide for each group of the inspecting party, as only five officers were left. All the others had been forced to leave the ship by the men, and the same conditions obtained on board the other battleships. On the whole, the revolution had been bloodless in Wilhelmshaven, four officers only losing their lives.

The first impression of the ward-room is unforgettable. Tables and chairs were still undamaged. Pictures of princes and admirals still hung on the walls. Sometimes even the Kaiser's portrait glared down in ferocious impotence upon the intruders. On one side of the room stood the German officers, with downcast eyes and lugubrious faces, silent except when the interpreter asked for information. Only one or two tried to preserve that stiff, unbending demeanour which we are wont to regard as typically Prussian. The stuffy atmosphere, the closed windows, the whispered consultations of the British officers arranging the details if the inspection, the stricken faces of the Germans, the silence of the ship's gangways, in which the singled footstep of an orderly made a hollow, lonely sound, all gave the impression of the preparations for some undistinguished suburban funeral, with the relatives waiting in the parlour for the body to be carried downstairs.

Mixed with the despondency of the German naval officers was a nervous curiosity as to what their treatment would be at our hands. There was, of course, not a glimmer of cordiality shown on our side, but at the same time the enemy was agreeably surprised to find himself neither hustled nor affronted. The Captain of one battleship, indeed, was so overwhelmed with the silent consideration for his feelings shown throughout the inspection that he stepped forward as they party was preparing to leave the ship and helped a British warrant officer on with his overcoat.

The situation of the crews was one of cynical curiosity. It was a condition of the inspection that no men should remain on board except those required to act as guides. The remainder were to leave the ship. In some cases this had been done; in others a fair number of men were still loafing about the deck with their hands in their pockets, some smoking cigars. As a result of emphatic protests by the Commission the German officers succeeded in clearing the decks of men and there was no repetition of this irregularity in Wilhelmshaven. No hostility at all was shown to the members of the Commission; in fact the German sailors showed them far greater respect than they did their own officers, one of whom had the humiliation of being addressed as "Kamerad" in our presence. A small percentage of the men showed signs of discipline and obedience, but the great majority were listless and slovenly in appearance and behaviour. Nevertheless there seemed to be a tacit agreement among all ranks that the work of the Commission must be made easy at all costs, and so domestic troubles were kept in the background during our stay in German waters. The officers made no secret of their intention to leave their ships, if they could, as soon as our task was completed. The men will drift away whenever it suits them to do so, and the remnants of the High Sea Fleet will fall an easy prey to time and the weather, unless, of course, the Allies have other intentions.

The results of neglect were already apparent on board most of the ships. Three of the battleships, having less than one hundred men on board, were in a filthy state, their brass-work all tarnished, decks littered with rubbish and boiler-rooms full of ashes, which nobody would clear away. The remainder, having still about two-thirds of their complement, were in better condition and there was little difficulty in carrying out the inspection. Among the light cruisers were the Konigsberg, in which Admiral Meurer had made his famous journey to the Firth of Forth to meet Admiral Beatty, and the Regensberg, already familiar to us and destined to accompany the Hercules through the Kiel Canal. She had sustained an injury to her propeller and was in dry dock for the time being. The commander informed us that she was one of the first ships to fall completely into the hands of the mutineers, who had burnt all her papers. After the first outburst, offices and men had come to some sort of agreement and she was again in a fairly serviceable condition, though of course disarmed. The Commission even had the unusual experience of being piped on board and the officers were most obliging. Altogether the light cruisers made a much better impression than the battleships.

When the inspection of the larger ships was over, visits were paid to a number of old torpedo-boats, which lay tied up alongside the pier in batches of five or six. All were dirty and evil-smelling. On the whole the demeanour of the officers was stiffer than on the larger ships, bordering at times on the comic. Perhaps they were offended at the very rapid rate of inspection, which was hardly flattering to their sense of their own importance. Last of all, a batch of mine-sweepers and auxiliary ships claimed attention. The latter were mostly British merchantmen which had the misfortune to be detained in German harbours at the beginning of the war. The Germans consistently followed the principle of converting such steamers into auxiliaries so that their own might be ready for the resumption of trade at the end of the war. The result has been other than was anticipated, for they now find themselves saddled with the task of restoring these merchantmen to their former condition. This work was already in progress and giant cranes were busy removing sea-plane sheds and other fittings from the deck. Some ships, such as Gifford, renamed Giffhorn, had been filled with barrels, logs, spars, cork and other buoyant material. They appear to have been used to discover mines by the simple process of bumping into them, which must have been rather exciting for the crew. If such a ship struck a mine it was expected that her cargo would keep her afloat while she limped home to tell the tale to the High Sea Fleet.

After two days of inspection there was little left for the Commission to see in Wilhelmshaven and it became necessary to arrange a series of excursions to the remoter naval stations. Our destroyers, which had hitherto ploughed along in the wake of the Hercules, now came into their own, for the channels to be navigated were winding and narrow. Under the envious eyes of their less fortunate colleagues the flying officers embarked one morning in the Verdun and sped down the now monotonous Jade to the sea. Their goal was Borkum, the island fortress and seaplane station at the mouth of the Ems, and as the low shores of the Frisian Islands, Wangeroog, Spiekeroog, Langeoog, Baltrum, Norderney and Juist came into view the thoughts of most turned to that now famous book "The Riddle of the Sands"[69], and the dark conspiracy hatched in the shed on little Memmert.

On the return journey the Verdun was held up by fog at the mouth of the Jade. This delay resulted in a change of plan, and very soon, to their great delight, the same lucky party found themselves on their way to Heligoland and

---

[69] Novel by Erskine Childers.

List, the latter an important seaplane station on the island of Sylt. From List they were conveyed to the airship station of Tondern, which had frequently suffered from the gallant attacks of our naval airmen. The last raid, made in the summer of 1918, had been completely successful and the party was able to bring back confirmation of the destruction of both sheds and Zeppelins.

The arrangements for these excursions to outlying places necessitated frequent visits from members of the German Commission, who seemed gradually to throw off a little of their despondency as they became involved in the settlement of details. Probably the fact of being definitely ordered to do something at a certain time was a welcome relief from the hopeless muddle of their own affairs. Still, it must have been a bitter contrast for them to leave their own derelict ships and be piped on board the Hercules with the most punctilious formality. Her starboard side was illuminated by night with a row of electric lamps and from the after-waist would come strains of music and the shuffle of dancing feet, or shrieks of laughter provoked by the antics of Charlie Chaplin on the screen. Bitter, too, must have been the atmosphere of cheerfulness, smartness and efficiency in comparison with the sulky squalor of Wilhelmshaven.

[The arrangement of these personally-conducted tours, as they were facetiously termed, owing to the fact that a German officer accompanied each party to negotiate with the local authorities at each port of call, proceeded apace, and hardly a day passed without the departure or return of one of the destroyers. Some places, such as inland airship-stations, were visited by car or train. Indeed, as one of the junior members of the Commission remarked later on, it was easier to reserve (and get) a special train gratis in Germany from anywhere to anywhere else, than to reserve a sleeping berth from Edinburgh to London. Among the places visited by train were Emden and Hamburg, where numerous small auxiliary craft were assembled. Their importance for the merchant shipping section of the Commission was, of course, even greater. On these occasions brief opportunities offered themselves of learning something about the local economic conditions. Food appeared to be sufficient, though not attractive. In spite of the great shortage of fats, no obvious cases of malnutrition were noticed, though observation was of necessity only casual. The children seemed about as lively as German children used to be before the war and the physique of the men was good. Of course it ought to be good, as the population hereabouts is largely seafaring and moreover the whole of northwest Germany is a rich agricultural district. Probably the very old and the very young are the real sufferers in these parts. In any case, it would be most unsafe to judge the condition of all Germany from a very superficial impression of the north-west.]

II. Hamburg

Hamburg was in a worse state of political confusion than any other town visited by the Commission. One of the three surviving cities of Germany, it had been a self-governing republic within the Empire, but apparently it was not sufficiently Republican to satisfy the taste of the sailors or workmen. With the help of a light cruiser, the Augsburg, of which the mutineers had obtained complete possession, so an officer of the German Commission informed us, the Senate had been overthrown and a new socialistic government set up.

A sharp distinction must be drawn between the naval and commercial ports. In the former there had been mutiny, followed by the overthrow of the naval and military authority without any definite end in view beyond a cessation of naval warfare; in the latter it was a case of revolt on the part of the labouring classes against the control of the capitalists, a process which was successfully completed with military assistance from the mutineers. Both these movements, of which the latter is the more extensive and formidable in its consequences, derived their direct successful impetus from the general recognition of Germany's impotence at sea and her military defeat on land, but the steady deterioration of economic conditions caused by the blockade had prepared a fruitful soil for the seeds of revolution.

Apart from the desirability of discovering the condition of Hamburg, it was essential to visit the dockyards in order to liberate the numerous British ships detained there. To save time the shipping commission went direct by special train, while the Vidette made the long journey by sea and river to bring them back the next day. The party spent one night in an hotel, whence they brought back favourable reports of the food supplied, though the sheets and towels were of paper, ingeniously worked up to resemble fine canvas. As at Wilhelmshaven, several British steamers had been converted into seaplane carriers and orders were at once given for their reconstruction and repair. Envious glances were cast at the mighty Bismarck, a huge Hamburg-America liner of over 50,000 tons, slowly nearing completion in the yards of Blohm and Voss, and the opinion was generally expressed that she would do very well to replace the Lusitania.

Scarcely had the shipping commission departed in the Vidette, when the Venetia arrived with a purely naval party, consisting of four British and two American officers. She had left Wilhelmshaven two days before with two German officers on board, one to act as pilot, the other to conduct local negotiations. Her first destination was Bremerhaven, which was reached in about three hours. The course was none too easy for a really big destroyer, as there are many hidden sandbanks between the estuaries of the Jade and the

Weser. Moreover, the position of the buoys and lightships were none too certain, as they had only been recently and hurriedly set out. Near the mouth of the Jade a buoy marked the wreck of the Yorck, a battle cruiser which struck a mine and sank there in 1915 on her return from a raid on the English coast. After turning at the angle of the two rivers, the Venetia entered the winding channel of the Weser and anchored about noon before the entrance to the great basin of the North German Lloyd, in which half-a-dozen giant liners were peacefully reposing. Motors were in waiting for the party, as the numerous small craft to be inspected were scattered in distant parts of the harbour. They were of little consequence and in two hours the inspection was complete. Next morning the Venetia slipped gently down the river and out to sea. As she turned west to round the shoals which separate the Weser from the Elbe, the Hercules was sighted astern, shaping the same course, but the two ships met only at Kiel, the Venetia being bound first for Hamburg. A brief call was made at Cuxhaven to inspect a few mine seekers and then began the long voyage to the Elbe, Hamburg being reached after dark.

The business of the Venetia was purely naval and so thoroughly did the Commission overhaul the Vulkan and Blohm and Voss yards that the existence of nearly seventy submarines, in various stages of construction, was brought to light. A report was also made on the condition of the new battle-cruiser Mackensen and various other warships of different types.

There was no evidence whatever of naval authority in Hamburg. Large numbers of mine-sweeping boats had come up the Elbe, because the crews preferred the attractions of a large town to the monotony of the naval stations, and it was some time before officers could be found to receive the Commission. The commander of the pecant Augsburg, which lay conveniently within point-blank range of the Venetia's after guns, had come up from Cuxhaven the previous day, and no one envied him his task. There was a delay of fully ten minutes while he argued with the crew, who at last trooped sullenly off the ship, whereupon the inspection was commenced and completed without further incident.

As all the vessels of the British flotilla passed through the Kiel Canal in both directions, a word or two of description will not be out of place. It runs for about sixty miles through perfectly flat country, uninteresting at the best of times and particularly lifeless in the pale December light. No ship was to be seen except an occasional barge or tug, but now and then a little cluster of people at some ferry raised wondering eyes as the British flagship flapped coldly past. The canal was widened and deepened just before the war, so that vessels drawing up to about thirty-five feet can use it. There are no locks except at each end, viz. Brunsbuttel and Holtenau. Ships of moderate size can pass one another almost anywhere, while there are particularly wide sections in which they can even turn round. Four or five tall railway bridges span the canal and chain ferries connect the roads that lead down to it. One of these bridges was built by prisoners of war and requires only the completion of the central span to be ready for traffic. The waterway is illuminated by night for the whole of its length and is perhaps most attractive under these conditions. By day the landscape is monotonous, the only interesting break being at Rendsburg, where the Eider River joins the Canal. From this point to Holtenau, on Kiel Bay, the banks are rather elevated, with occasional clusters of trees and one or two large country mansions.

III. Kiel

Kiel Bay, where the Hercules and her attendant destroyers were happily united, is a pretty place. The landlocked harbour has hilly shores, with pleasant villas dotting the slopes. Even in winter the bay showed signs of life. Ferry steamers crossed frequently from shore to shore and small pleasure boats were rowed cautiously round the Hercules to give the curious a glimpse of the invaders. It is an ill wind that blows nobody good, and like the photographers of Wilhelmshaven the boatmen of Kiel saw a chance to earn an honest penny. Another source of income to them was the steady stream of released Allied prisoners who were lucky enough to sight our ships and make their way down to the shore. Four British soldiers were picked up at Wilhelmshaven and the Venetia brought back seventy from Hamburg, while twenty-one French and seventeen Belgian prisoners were taken aboard the flagship in Kiel. It was difficult to say who were the more delighted, the prisoners to be free or the sailors to receive them.

Practically every German ship in Kiel was obsolete, except perhaps a couple of light cruisers, and the inspection of surface-craft was tedious to the last degree. The harbour was choked with a mass of old torpedo-boats. One or two new destroyers were under repair and for that reason had not been sent to Scapa. Only in the submarine department was anything of importance discovered, with the result that a number of boards under construction will have to be destroyed and certain others, which were said to be too much in need of repair to be able to travel, have now recovered sufficiently to proceed into captivity.

The general attitude of the men in Kiel was less servile than in Wilhelmshaven, while the officers, though equally powerless, were more inclined to quibble over details. Once or twice the representatives of the Soldiers' and Workmen's Council, who were generally visible in the background, attempted to assert themselves, but were of course completely ignored. At one point, where the crowd of sailors and labourers on the quay was becoming rather dense and threatened to incommode the inspecting officers, a sailor with a white band round his arm pushed them back shouting, entirely on his own responsibility, "The English are going to break off negotiations at once if you don't stand back!" The warning was completely effective, whereas the authority of the German commander who acted as guide carried no weight whatsoever.

While the Hercules lay in Kiel Bay the same procedure was adopted as in Wilhelmshaven. First of all the ships in the harbour and the dockyard were inspected; then the destroyers were dispatched to supervise the disarmament of outlying stations. One party visited the flying-stations on the island of Rugen and at Warnemunde. Another, consisting mainly of gunnery experts, waded through the mud of Arusund to inspect the dismantled fortifications of the Little Belt.

Only once did we meet the Prussian of our dreams. He was a lieutenant-commander in the submarine service and he wore the highest distinction, the cross of the order of Pour le Merite, presumably for the destruction of Allied merchantmen. His business on board the Hercules was to deliver certain letters to Admiral Browning and to wait for an answer; in the meantime he was invited to come under cover as it was raining. It would appear that he was too proud to accept even this trifling hospitality from an enemy ship; at any rate he bluntly refused and remained standing to attention at the top of the ladder with his portfolio clenched under his left arm. One or two officers who happened to come on board gazed on him in astonishment and as the rain was steadily trickling from the peak of his cap and the end of his nose they naturally repeated the invitation to come in out of the wet, but all to no purpose. A very snappy "Nein!" was all they got for their pains, so he was left to pose in all his dignity, while the ship's band played merrily in the background. It was a very wet and disconsolate Hun that received orders half-an-hour later to pilot the Venetia to Bremen on another hunt for hidden submarines.

This was the last noteworthy incident of the voyage and on Wednesday, December 19th, the little flotilla, now strengthened by the light cruiser Constance, passed through the Kiel Canal once more and hurried home to the Firth of Forth, just in time for a well-earned Christmas leave.

IV. Bremerhaven

The recent drastic amendments to the naval terms of the Armistice, which now include the destruction, under Allied supervision, of all submarines not yet completed, is a direct result of the investigations of the Allied Naval Armistice Commission in German ports. While the Hercules lay in Wilhelmshaven Roads, her destroyer escort, Verdun, Viceroy, Venetia and Vidette, was busily employed in conveying small parties of experts to the ports that could not easily be reached by a large vessel. Probably the most fruitful of these expeditions was the voyage of the Venetia to Bremerhaven and Hamburg, which resulted in the discovery of about seventy hidden submarines and the rescue of sixty-eight British prisoners of war.

With four British and two American members of the Commission on board, she left her anchorage near the Hercules on the morning of Monday, December 9th. A German officer accompanied her as far as Cuxhaven as a pilot, and another remained attached throughout the journey as a representative of the German Commission. It was his duty to introduce the inspecting officers to the local authorities at each port of call and to make the necessary arrangements in advance.

As we sped down the broad Jade the sun pierced the mist which had enveloped us relentlessly every day, and it was easy to pick up the buoys that marked the channel, including the small black one marking the wreck of the Yorck. Just south of the Minsener Sand lightship, with Roter Sand in line due north, we turned smartly to the south-east and made for the Hoheweg lightship, which lies at the entrance to the Weser. As there were few of us on board who had not read "The Riddle of the Sands," the appearance of these names stirred a responsive chord of recognition in our memories. Our interest in the charts that lay before us was still further stimulated by an occasional disagreement between the two German officers as to the correct position of some of the buoys, which were not always where they were expected. The explanation given was that they had been removed during the war and had only just been replaced, none too accurately, by the Workmen's and Soldiers' Council, partly for our special benefit, partly for the expected general resumption of navigation. Moreover the German officers quite cheerfully proposed to take the Venetia by the short cuts they themselves used with their own smaller boats, either forgetting or being unwilling to recognise the obvious disparity in size. However, the Captain was taking no risks and stuck everywhere to the deepest and most regular channels. Luckily the morning was bright and free from fog and so shortly before one o'clock the Venetia dropped anchor off the entrance to the Kaiser Wilhelm basin at Bremerhaven. Behind the wall could be seen at least half-a-dozen enormous vessels of the North German Lloyd, and presently a tug, manned by sailors of that line came alongside to take the Commission ashore. The immediate impression was one of greater order than in the naval dockyards. Bremerhaven is purely commercial and the naval grievances seem hardly to have arisen. Indeed, there were only about a score of small auxiliary vessels in the harbour.

A little group of children thronged round us as we landed, but they were sternly kept in check by a real Schutzman, wearing a real spiked helmet. Three motors were waiting and two officers of the Commission got into each and were driven at breakneck speed to the more distant basins where the boats lay. This gave us our first glimpse of civil life. It was a cold December afternoon and the streets looked lifeless, except where the electric cars were running. There seemed to be little or no display in the shops, except in the superfluous trades, such as cheap jewellery. Little food was to be seen exposed for sale beyond a few roots and vegetables, but of course observation from a rapidly moving car was very limited. Adult faces were everywhere despondent, but the children showed a lively interest and followed us in little bands whenever we had occasion to walk from one wharf to another. Nowhere did we see any sign of hostility. The sailors and labourers revealed the same officious anxiety to show us everything as at Willemshaven, while the officers were reserved and correct in their behaviour. Work was in progress here and there, but only in a desultory way, and the general atmosphere was of profound depression.

After the inspection followed another breakneck ride over the rough setts of the streets back to the quay where the tug was waiting. The journey was completed without accident, except for a burst tyre, which gave one party a walk of about half-a-mile. The solitary policeman was still on duty and roused himself to activity as the children once more gathered round. Once on board, a good wash and a solid tea removed the fatigue of a dull afternoon.

---

1. The Author – Second Lieutenant Officer Gilbert Waterhouse
2. Also known as "The Blue Max"

Chapter VII

The Aftermath and the Survivors

The marriage took place yesterday at Killiney Church of Professor Gilbert Waterhouse (T.C.D.), and Miss M. E. Woods, daughter of Sir Robert Woods, M.P., and Lady Woods. The photographs show (left) the bride and bridegroom and (right) Sir Robert and Lady Woods.

Gilbert and Molly met after the War. Their courtship speeded up by the combined efforts of Molly's parents and the Provost of Trinity College, Dr, Mehaffy. Dinners, picnics and similar devices led swiftly to the romantic involvement of these two most compatible young people, and the engagement was greeted with delight by Gilbert's parents. They were married in 1921, in Killiney Parish Church in Ballybrack.

My father continued at Trinity College until 1933, when he was appointed Professor of German The Queen's University of Belfast and we took up residence at 92 Malone Road, Belfast.

Hugh Waterhouse M.C. survived the war and was equally blessed. He returned to his studies and graduated from St. John's College, Cambridge, as his brother had done, and found happiness in his teaching career and his marriage to Betty Crabtree in Lytham-St. Annes.

Jack, Bobby and Patricia grew up and prospered with their own spouses, but they never forgot the much-loved brother and uncles they had lost, and the War and the Rebellion left them all with a great feeling of the responsibility they bore to try to make the world a better place for those who followed.

I have told this story, insofar as I can, entirely in the words of those who were at the heart of the events which impinged on and shaped their lives – the First World War and within it the "Easter Rising" in Dublin in 1916, perhaps more commonly known as the Irish Rebellion. But it has raised in my own mind the need to study more closely what the consequences were for my own generation, and specifically how it reflected on myself and my two sisters, Margaret and Elizabeth Waterhouse, born of these intelligent and devoted parents who had nothing in common in their own parentage.

My mother, Molly Woods, always described herself as Anglo-Irish – to her it meant being born within "The Pale" narrowly defined by County Dublin and the stretch of coast from Dalkey to Drogheda.

She knew how that defined her. Her identity was firmly Irish, her loyalty was firmly to the British Crown. She went, as many of her friends did, to boarding school in England, and from there to Cambridge University. She spoke a form of English that had been brought to Ireland in Elizabethan times and survived there in a kind of special isolation.

My father, Gilbert Waterhouse, had another kind of ancestral pride, that he was of pure Anglo-Saxon origin, as the name indeed implies, unsullied by the Norman invasion or any other influence on his deep Yorkshire/Lancashire inheritance.

Where did all this leave the three daughters of this fortuitous union?

My eldest sister, Margaret, felt her Lancashire roots were deep, she had known and loved my father's extended family from an early age, when my father had still felt nervous in Dublin and took his family to his mother's home for some of the stormy 1920s. School in Wales had been followed by success at Newnham College, Cambridge, and her joy was complete when her academic Ulster husband was called to a Chair at Manchester University. My second sister, Elizabeth, followed her mother in her love of all things Irish, unhesitatingly chose Trinity College, Dublin for her degree, and embraced all the places that had been so dear to the Woods family. And while romance eventually took her with an English husband to the West Indies, she always pined for Dublin.

Where did all this leave me? Still Anglo-Irish, but not quite, gradually more and more Ulster-Scots, by lineage and environment, being transplanted from Dublin to Belfast at four years old. I am happy and proud to have the Shaws, the Maxwells and the Gambles of the Ards Peninsula as my ancestors, and to have married a man whose forebears trod a similar route from Scotland to North Antrim. But at school in Wales I felt a hybrid, because there I was laughed at for my Irishness, while at home in the streets of Belfast I can still be asked what part of England do I come from?

Somehow my whole life has been defined by the few years in which my Irish uncles fought for their country, England, while my English roots sought to find an acceptable soil to flourish and grow in their adopted land, Ireland.

Appendix A - Shaw Family

	Judge James Johnston Shaw
Birth	1 Apr 1845
Death	27 Apr 1910
Occupation	1869 appointed Chair of Metaphysics and Ethics at Magee College and County Court Judge, Recorder of Belfast
Education	Belfast Academy and Queen's College, Belfast
Father	John Maxwell Shaw (- 1851)
Mother	Anne Johnston (1814 - 1900)

	Mary Elizabeth Maxwell
Birth	1842
Death	20 Jan 1908
Father	William Maxwell
Mother	Sarah Gamble (1805 - 1867)

	Margaret Gamble Maxwell Shaw	
Birth	3 April 1872	Londonderry
Death	28 Sep 1949	Killiney, Co Dublin
Spouse	Sir Robert Woods	

	James Rowan Shaw
Birth	20 May 1880
Death	23 Feb 1916

	William Maxwell Shaw
Birth	19 Apr 1882
Death	28 May 1917

Appendix B - Woods Family

Sir Robert Woods		
Birth	27 April 1865	Tullamore
Death	Sep 1938	Killiney, Co Dublin
Burial		Dean's Grange
Occupation	Ear, Nose and Throat Surgeon	
Education	Methodist College and Trinity College, Dublin	
Religion	Church of Ireland	
Father	Christopher Woods (1816 - 1894)	
Mother	Dorothea Lowe (- 1911)	

Margaret Gamble Maxwell Shaw		
Birth	3 April 1872	Londonderry
Death	28 Sep 1949	Killiney, Co Dublin
Spouse	Sir Robert Woods	

Mary Elizabeth Woods		
Birth	11 Aug 1895	Dublin
Death	13 Nov 1980	Belfast
Spouse	Prof Gilbert Waterhouse	
Marriage	Aug 1920	Killiney Parish Church

Thornley Stoker Woods		
Birth	1896	Dublin
Death	30 Oct 1916	France

John Lowe Woods		
Birth	24 Jan 1899	Dublin
Death	29 March 1956	Ipoh
Spouse	Lydia Barton Sheehan	
Marriage	1928	

Robert Rowan Woods		
Birth	28 May 1902	Dublin
Death	1971	Dublin
Spouse	Margaret Rosita Roper	
Marriage	19 Apr 1934	Christ Church, Leeson Park, Dublin

Patricia Marjory Woods		
Birth	5 March 1904	Dublin
Death	10 Oct 1997	Dublin
Spouse	Rev Canon William Cecil Procter	
Marriage	5 Sep 1935	Killiney Parish Church, Ballybrack

Appendix C – Wadsworth Family

Arthur and George were brothers, the sons of Walter Wadsworth, whose father Daniel emigrated to New Zealand c. 1861. Daniel was himself the son of Daniel Wadsworth, snr and Elizabeth Derbyshire and grandson of John Jackson and Mary Wadsworth. This John Jackson was the father of Sarah Helen (Nellie) wife of Harold Waterhouse. Before he emigrated Daniel Wadsworth, who was born in Irlam, Lancashire, married Catherine Synott in St. Nicholas Church, Liverpool on 27 Aug. 1857. They settled in Otago, New Zealand, and are believed to be buried in Northern Cemetery, Dunedin.

Their children were:
    1. Mary Ann d. date unknown
    2. Sarah d. date unknown
    3. Horace Piers d. 12 Apr. 1966, Ocean Grove, Dunedin
    4. James d. 4 Apr. 1922
    5. Walter b. 1865 d. date unknown, 106 Shetland St., Kaikorai, Dunedin
    6. Daniel b.6 July 1866, Maori Hill, Otago. d. Dec. 1948 Woodlands, Southland, N.Z.

It would appear that there was then a second family, mother unknown, consisting of:
    7. Helen b. 25 June, 1874, Dunedin appearing in the letters as Helen Gibbs
    8. Moretta, b. 7 May 1876, Dunedin. D. date unknown
    9. Elizabeth b. 23 May, 1877, living in Port Chalmers, Dunedin, d. 23 Dec. 1945, appearing in the letters as Bessie Bell
    10. Peter b abt. 1878, d. 8 Mar. 1879 in Dunedin
    11. Thomas b. abt 1882, Mount Cargill, Dunedin, d. 23 Dec. 1921, Dunedin
    12. John, b abt 1886, d. 5 July, 1899, Dunedin

This means that Helen Gibbs and Bessie Bell were cousins of Sarah (Nellie) Waterhouse and aunts of Arthur and George.

Arthur was born on 13 Apr. 1893 and left N.Z for Melbourne, Australia approx. 12 years before the WW1. He married Isabella before leaving but there were no children. He served in the 27th Australian Army Service Corps. He died on 6th Nov. 1918.

George was born on 11 Dec., 1896 and served as a driver in the 4th Batt. N.Z. Rifle Brigade. He died on 29 Aug. 1918.

It would seem that Arthur certainly died in the 'flu epidemic of 1918. How George met his death is not clear from family records. Isabella refers to a "brother" who also died, but it is not clear whether she is referring to her own brother or to George.

HE whom this scroll commemorates was numbered among those who, at the call of King and Country, left all that was dear to them, endured hardness, faced danger, and finally passed out of the sight of men by the path of duty and self-sacrifice, giving up their own lives that others might live in freedom.

Let those who come after see to it that his name be not forgotten.

Bibliography

THE GRAPHIC Souvenir of the German Navy's Surrender pub. The Graphic, Tallis House, London, E.C.4.

SINN FEIN REBELLION HANDBOOK, compiled by the Weekly *Irish Times*, Dublin.

POEMS BY HILDA, printed by Charles William Deacon and Co., London 1907.

OCCASIONAL PAPERS by James Johnston Shaw pub. Hodges Figgis and Co. Ltd. 104 Grafton Street 1910.

AN IRISHMAN IN MALAYA by D.E. Moreton pub. by Volturna Press 1977.

COLLEGE OF ST. COLUMBA ROLL OF HONOUR pub. by the Old Columban Society, Dublin.

TRINITY IN WAR AND REVOLUTION 1912-1923 by Tomas Irish, pub. Royal Irish Academy.

REPORT OF WORK DONE BY ST. JOHN'S AMBULANCE BRIGADE DURING THE SINN FEIN REBELLION APRIL – MAY 1916, published by John Falconer, 53 Upper Sackville Street, Dublin 1916.